NAMES
of GOD

EXPLORING GOD'S CHARACTER

COUNTRYMAN®

A Division of Thomas Nelson Publishers

THOMAS NELSON
Since 1798

NASHVILLE   DALLAS   MEXICO CITY   RIO DE JANEIRO

CONTENTS

PART 1: NAMES OF GOD

1 Alpha 2

2 Her Seed 4

3 The Door 6

4 Jesus 8

5 The God Who Sees Me 12

6 Lord 14

7 Servant 17

8 The Way 20

9 The Truth 23

10 The Life 25

11 Teacher 28

12 The Root, the Vine, the Branch, and the Cup 32

13 Eternal God 36

14 The Morning Star 38

15 Rock 41

16 Holy Spirit 44

17 Living Water 48

18 The Gentle Whisper 52

19 Last Adam 54

20 Redeemer 56

21 Merciful God 59

22 Like an Eagle 62

23 Author and Editor 64

24 The Great Shepherd 66

25 Lamb 69

26 Immanuel—God with Us 73

27 Potter 75

28 Abba, Father 77

29 Creator 81

30 Owner of the Cattle on a Thousand Hills 84

31 Lion of the Tribe of Judah 87

32 A Consuming Fire 90

33 Man of Sorrows 93

34 El Shaddai 96

35 Advocate 100

36 Faithful Witness 102

37 Bridegroom 104

38 Prince of Peace 107

39 Living Bread 111

40 The Word 114

41 Rose of Sharon 117

42 Holy, Holy, Holy 119

43 Friend of Tax Collectors and Sinners 122

44 Omega 125

Appendix: *Join All the Glorious Names!* 127

Notes 130

PART 2: Attributes of God

1 Immanuel 132

2 Christ the Lord 133

3 Faithful Witness 134

4 Hope 135

5 Holy 136

6 Shepherd 137

7 Advocate 138

8 Prince of Peace 139

9 Gift of God 140

10 Firstborn over All Creation 141

11 Son of Man 142

12 Jesus 143

13 Author of Our Faith 144

14 Light of the World 145

15 Deliverer 146

16 High Priest 147

17 Redeemer 148

18 The Living Stone 149

19 King of Kings 150

20 Mediator 151

21 Savior 152

22 My Beloved Son 153

23 The Way, Truth, and Life 154

24 Lamb of God 155

25 Good Shepherd 156

26 Bread of Life 157

27 Word 158

28 Alpha & Omega 159

29 Resurrection 160

30 Messiah 161

Hallelujah Chorus 162

Notes 163

PART 3: PROMISES OF GOD

1 Jesus Is Your Savior 166

2 Jesus Is Your Lord 168

3 Jesus Is Your Love 171

4 Jesus Is Your Peace 174

5 Jesus Is Your Forgiveness 177

6 Jesus Is Your Righteousness 180

7 Jesus Is Your Deliverer 183

8 Jesus Is Your Fellowship 185

9 Jesus Is Your Example 188

10 Jesus Is Your Companion 190

11 Jesus Is Your Brother 192

12 Jesus Is Your Security 194

13 Jesus Is Your Sufficiency 198

14 Jesus Is Your Everything 201

PART 1

NAMES *of* GOD

1   ALPHA

Scripture: Genesis 1:1–2; John 1:1–14

> In the beginning God . . .
>
> Genesis 1:1

> In the beginning was the Word, and the Word was with God,
> and the Word was God. He was with God in the beginning.
>
> John 1:1–2

> I am the *Alpha* . . . , the First . . . , the Beginning.
>
> Revelation 22:13

Time had a beginning. Creation had a beginning. We had a beginning. Civilizations have a beginning. Books have a beginning. All of the endeavors we would undertake have their beginning.

But God? God has no beginning. Before any other beginning began, God was. "Before Abraham was born, I am!" declared Jesus (John 8:58). Why, then, would the eternal God have named himself Alpha, the first letter of the Greek alphabet, the beginning? It must have been because God is the great Beginner of all other beginnings! "Through him all things were made; without him nothing was made that has been made" (John 1:3).

Christ, to thee, with God the Father,

And, O Holy Ghost, to thee,

Hymn and chant and high thanksgiving,

And unwearied praises be:

Honor, glory, and dominion,

And eternal victory,

Evermore and evermore.

—Aurelius Clemens Prudentius (348–c. 410)

Alpha God, we lay before you that which we will attempt to begin this day. We acknowledge that without you, all our attempts at beginnings are in vain. We can't see what will result from that which we now begin. Apprehension is mixed with our enthusiasm. We place it before you, Alpha God, knowing that you see not just the beginning but the whole.

We worship you; we build our lives upon you, our Alpha God, who is truly without beginning.

2 HER SEED

Scripture: Genesis 3:1–20; Galatians 3:19, 23–29

> The Lord God said to the serpent . . . I will put enmity between
> you and the woman, and between your seed and *her seed*; he
> shall bruise your head, and you shall bruise his heel.
>
> Genesis 3:14–15 rsv

> What, then, was the purpose of the law? It was added because
> of transgressions until *the Seed* to whom the promise referred
> had come.
>
> Galatians 3:19

A seed is a promise of what is to come. Tiny and insignificant in appearance, it nonetheless contains within it the complete and particular genetic code for the life it is intended to produce.

The eternal God, who requires no other for origin or completion, desires creatures who will freely choose to love him. These creatures have to be able to choose to love, or not, for love of God with its accompanying obedience must be freely offered, or it is not love. It didn't take the earliest humans long to choose the "or not." And humans have been compounding their choices in the "or not" column ever since.

But Eve's risk-taking God persists. The love and compassion

that we tend to see more readily in our reading of the New Testament begins here in Genesis 3. The humans created in God's own image have just shattered any possibility of the sort of loving communion God wants with them. In the presence of Adam and Eve, God speaks to Satan's instrument, the serpent, telling it how this story is going to end. From now on, God says, there is enmity—irreconcilable differences—between Satan's seed and the seed of Eve. From Eve's offspring will come the Seed (Gal. 3:19), Jesus Christ. Satan will bruise the heel of Eve's Seed. The damage will be costly and painful, but not like the fatal bruising of Satan's head that will be accomplished by Eve's Seed, Jesus.

A seed is a treasure. But this treasure must die and be buried for its potential to be realized. Jesus said, "Unless a kernel of wheat falls to the ground and dies, it remains only a single seed. But if it dies, it produces many seeds" (John 12:24). Jesus' death and resurrection for us dealt a crushing blow to Satan's head. The ending of this story is told with certainty in Genesis 3. Satan loses! Jesus' death and resurrection for us produced many seeds with his DNA. We, Eve's other offspring, owe our eternal life to the death of her Seed. The hymn writer invites:

> O seed of Israel's chosen race now ransomed from the fall,
> Hail him who saves you by his grace, and crown him Lord of all!
> —Edward Perronet, 1780

Lord Jesus Christ, you are the seed promised to Eve in her darkest hour. You are Eve's hope, and you are our hope. We praise you, Seed of Eve.

3   THE DOOR

Scripture: Exodus 12:7; John 10:1–10

> I am *the door*. Whoever comes in through Me shall be saved;
> they will go in and out and find pasture.
>
> John 10:9 BV

They were very ordinary doors, set in very ordinary houses. Their uniqueness lay only in the fact that their frames had been freshly painted with lamb's blood.

These doors closed out the cold night air and the turmoil and pain of the outside world. The angel of death was engaged in a terrible mission that night. Relentlessly, one by one, he summoned the firstborn in all the other houses. But he would not violate the closed doors framed in lamb's blood. Within these doors were peace and a quiet expectancy that could not be understood by those outside.

The next morning, many walked out through those same blood-framed doors. They left behind their slavery. The open door led them to opportunity and freedom.

Jesus Christ is the Door those doors of long ago were pointing toward. The frame is painted with his blood.

Jesus Christ is the Door that closes out that which would destroy us, providing us peace and safety as we take refuge behind him.

Jesus Christ is the Door that opens up to us opportunity, freedom, and "life . . . to the full" (John 10:10).

Today we claim his protection. We claim the abundant life to which he would lead us. And we may claim the Lamb's blood on his doorframe.

We love you, Lord Jesus, our Door. It is through you we have gained our entrance. Now enter us, we pray, and fill us with yourself this day.

4 JESUS

SCRIPTURE: MATTHEW 1:18–24; REVELATION 22:20–21

She will give birth to a son, and you are to give him the name
Jesus, because he will save his people from their sins.

MATTHEW 1:21

Above his head they placed the written charge against him:
THIS IS *JESUS*, THE KING OF THE JEWS.

MATTHEW 27:37

Therefore God exalted him to the highest place
and gave him the name that is above every name,
that at the name of *Jesus* every knee should bow,
in heaven and on earth and under the earth,
and every tongue confess that *Jesus* Christ is Lord,
to the glory of God the Father.

PHILIPPIANS 2:9–11

By faith in the name of *Jesus*, this man whom you see and
know was made strong. It is *Jesus'* name and the faith that
comes through him that has given this complete healing to
him, as you can all see.

ACTS 3:16

He who testifies to these things says, "Yes, I am coming soon."
Amen. Come, Lord *Jesus*. The grace of the Lord *Jesus* be with
God's people. Amen.

REVELATION 22:20–21

*M*any names, when traced to their origin, describe the job or occupation of the one so named: Smith, Taylor (tailor), Baker, Butler, Fisher, Carpenter. The Gospel writer Matthew records a dream in which Joseph was told to name the son his wife-to-be, Mary, would bear Jesus, because of the job he would do. He would save his people from their sin. Jesus is the Savior.

Sin sometimes comes in a gilded wrapping, but when viewed for what it is, it is never a pretty subject. Sin is ugly. It is a slap in the face of God. It cannot go unpunished.

Greek and Roman mythology is full of tales of how the gods punished mortals for various sins committed against them.

Arachne was a young Greek girl whose pride was her downfall. She thought she could weave more skillfully than the goddess Athena and challenged the goddess to a competition. As a punishment, Arachne and her descendants were changed forever into the form of spiders.

Sisyphus had the audacity to trick the gods into giving him something he wanted. For his punishment, he was made to push a huge boulder up a steep hill. Every time it almost reached the top, it would slip from his hands and roll back down, and he was made to roll it back up again, and again, and again—eternally.

Tantalus murdered his son in a misguided attempt to make an offering to the gods. The gods punished him by making him stand forever in water up to his neck. But he was never able to quench his thirst, for whenever he bent to drink, the water receded. Above his head hung branches loaded with fruit, but whenever he tried to pick one, the branch bent out of his reach.

You and I have sinned. We deserve eternal punishment, just as did the sinful humans depicted in the Greek myths. But unlike the gods, which are creations of human imagination, the real God truly loves the people he made, even though they are sinful. So Jesus came.

Jesus himself wore our pride to the cross. Unlike Arachne, we won't need to wear its consequences throughout eternity.

Jesus himself carried the huge boulder of our sin to the cross—and rolled it away forever.

Jesus freed us from our sin by his death on the cross and put living water eternally within our reach.

There is power in the name of Jesus. It is the power to forgive sins and to change lives. The blind man, Bartimaeus, received his sight when he called on the name of Jesus (Mark 10:46–52). Peter and John invoked the power of the name of Jesus, and a lame man began to walk and leap and praise God (Acts 3:1–16). A meeting with the Jesus he had been persecuting completely turned around the life of the man Saul of Tarsus. And there will come a day when every knee in heaven, on earth, and under the earth will bow, acknowledging at last that Jesus Christ is Lord.

> I lay my sins on Jesus, the spotless Lamb of God;
> He bears them all, and frees us from the accursed load:
> I bring my guilt to Jesus, to wash my crimson stains
> White in his blood most precious, 'till not a spot remains.
>
> —HORATIUS BONAR, 1843

It is at your name that we bow today, Lord Jesus, and our tongues confess you as Lord. To God be all glory!

5 | THE GOD WHO SEES ME

SCRIPTURE: GENESIS 16; 21:8–20

> She gave this name to the LORD who spoke to her: "You are *the God who sees me*," for she said, "I have now seen the One who sees me."
>
> GENESIS 16:13

*D*uring the construction of the National Cathedral in Washington, D.C., a visitor stopped to watch an elderly stone carver working painstakingly at his craft. The visitor noted that when this particular piece of carving was put in place, it would be next to the wall, where no one could see it.

"Why are you working so hard on something no one will ever see?" asked the amazed onlooker.

"God will see it," replied the carver.

Sometimes it is a little unsettling to realize that ours is a God who is all-seeing! We'd rather put our mistakes and blemishes in the shadows, in a corner, against a wall—anything to get them out of sight. At times we succeed in hiding that which we wish to hide from other people, but we never can hide it from God's penetrating, purifying gaze:

The eyes of the LORD are everywhere,
> keeping watch on the wicked and the good. (Prov. 15:3)

But there are other times, when, like Hagar, we marvel with gratitude at the God who sees. The problems we encounter that no one else seems to understand—God sees.

He will not let your foot slip—
> he who watches over you will not slumber;
indeed, he who watches over Israel
> will neither slumber nor sleep.

The LORD watches over you—
> the LORD is your shade at your right hand;
the sun will not harm you by day,
> nor the moon by night,

The LORD will keep you from all harm—
> he will watch over your life;
The LORD will watch over your coming and going
> both now and forevermore. (Ps. 121:3–8)

Our Seeing God penetrates and purges the dark corners of our sinfulness. Our Seeing God protects and preserves us from danger. Our Seeing God feels our private pain along with us.

Seeing God, we praise your name! Today we trust you with the thoughts of our hearts and the works of our hands that are unseen by others. Today we trust you with the future we cannot see, grateful that you will see us into it and through it.

6 LORD

O LORD, our Lord,
> how majestic is your name in all the earth!

> PSALM 8:1

And the glory of the LORD will be revealed,
> and all mankind together will see it.
>> For the mouth of the LORD has spoken.

> ISAIAH 40:5

On his robe and on his thigh he has this name written: . . .
LORD OF LORDS.

> REVELATION 19:16

The title *lord* has lost some of its impact in our egalitarian culture. In feudal society, a lord was a man of high rank, perhaps even a king. He might have been the proprietor of a manor or a man who had mastery in a given field. The relationship of servants to their lord was a formal, respectful one. The title *lord* demanded unquestioning obedience from the servant.

The disciple Peter's outburst, "Surely not, Lord! . . . I have never eaten anything impure or unclean" (Acts 10:14), was a contradiction in terms. To say "surely not" in response to his Lord's invitation was to deny lordship. That what Peter was asked to do ran counter to the customs and traditions with which he had been brought up was not a consideration.

But before we are too hard on Peter, we need to consider our own responses:

"But, Lord . . ."

"Not me, Lord . . ."

"No, Lord."

"Lord, why?"

Sometimes our outbursts are spoken, sometimes not. Our Lord has every right to say to his disciples and to us, "Why do you call me, 'Lord, Lord,' and do not do what I say?" (Luke 6:46).

The problem with feudal lords was that they were not all-knowing, so they sometimes made unwise demands. Some did not truly love their servants, so they misused the power of their lordship.

We need not fear that kind of abuse of power. The One we call Lord loved us enough to give his own life for us. He is all-knowing and all-wise. The commands he gives us spring from that love and that wisdom and demand our obedience. One servant wrote of this Lord:

Were the whole realm of nature mine,
That were a present far too small;
Love so amazing, so divine,
Demands my soul, my life, my all.

—Isaac Watts, 1709

Lord of Lords, today we bow before you, acknowledging your greatness and goodness.
Accept now our worship, we pray.

SERVANT

SCRIPTURE: JOHN 13:1–17; PHILIPPIANS 2:1–11; ISAIAH 42:1

Here is my *servant*, whom I uphold,
    my chosen one in whom I delight;
I will put my Spirit on him
    and he will bring justice to the nations.

ISAIAH 42:1; CF. MATTHEW 12:18

Jesus knew that the Father had put all things under his power,
and that he had come from God and was returning to God;
so he got up from the meal, took off his outer clothing, and
wrapped a towel around his waist. After that, he poured water
into a basin and began to wash his disciples' feet, drying them
with the towel that was wrapped around him.

JOHN 13:3–5

Your attitude should be the same as that of Christ Jesus:

Who, being in very nature God,
    did not consider equality with God something to be grasped,
but made himself nothing,
    taking the very nature of a *servant*,
    being made in human likeness.

PHILIPPIANS 2:5–7

$\mathcal{T}$he dinner guests all arrived on foot. Open sandals were all that protected their feet from the dusty roads. Customarily, a servant from the host's household would have met them at the door and washed and dried their feet. That nicety had been overlooked this particular night. It was to a borrowed room that this group had come to observe the Passover Feast. One of the men seated at the table slipped from his place, stripped down to the short tunic, which was all a servant would have worn, and wrapped a towel about himself. He went around the group without a word, kneeling at the feet of each of the men present, and washed and dried them. Until he reached the place of the man called Peter. Undoubtedly all of the men realized the incongruity of the situation—they probably all felt a little sheepish. Here was the man they called Lord and Teacher performing a most menial task for them! But their sheepishness had rendered them speechless. Except for Peter.

"Not my feet!" Peter protested.

But Jesus was insistent. "Unless I wash you, you have no part with me" (John 13:8).

Who was this guest-turned-servant? He was truly God. But he did not grasp his God-ness. He set it aside and submitted to servanthood.

His was not a conditional submission: I'll submit to you if you submit to me; or I'll serve you if you'll give me lots of sympathy for doing this miserable job; or I'll do it in exchange for a generous supply of credit, attention, and pats on the back.

Most of us don't understand servanthood very well. Jesus laid aside his God-ness to help us understand. Being a servant means considering others better than oneself. It means looking out for the other person's interests and needs first. Being a servant means being obedient. It means attributing all credit and honor to the one served. To truly serve takes the truest sort of nobility.

The One whose name is above every name knelt and washed dirty feet to set an example for us.

> May the mind of Christ my Savior
> > Live in me from day to day
> By His love and power controlling
> > All I do and say.
>
> May His beauty rest upon me
> > As I seek the lost to win.
> And may they forget the channel
> > Seeing only Him.[1]

—KATE B. WILKINSON (1859–1928)

Servant Lord, You have shown us how to serve. Now open our eyes to the feet that need washing, the wounds that need binding, and the burdens that need lifting this day. May we wash, bind, and lift as though they were your feet, your wounds, and your burdens.

$\approx|8$ THE WAY

SCRIPTURE: JOHN 14:1–6; HEBREWS 10:19–25; PSALM 1

The blood of Jesus, . . . a new and living *way* opened for us.

HEBREWS 10:19–20

I am *the way* . . . No one comes to the Father except through me.

JOHN 14:6

The lone mountain climber, partway up Mount Fuji, reached a fork in the trail. One of the trails was marked by a sign, its message painted boldly and clearly. This was the way the climber chose to follow. The mountain climber was a scholar, conversant in a number of classical and modern languages. But he didn't know Japanese and thus couldn't read the message on that boldly painted sign. The message read: "Danger! This way should be attempted only by the most skilled and experienced climbers." Having taken the wrong way, this climber fell and lost his life.

Signs clutter our streets and highways. Sometimes they amuse us; sometimes they disgust us; sometimes they provide useful information. The intent of the one who places a sign is that we will pursue a certain prescribed course of action or follow in a certain way.

Because of sin, we have lost our way. We are without direction or purpose and have no hope of finding reconciliation with the Father. The bridge is out. There is no crossing the deep chasm created by sin.

But Jesus, like a bold signpost, declares authoritatively, "I am the way . . . No one comes to the Father except through me." Then Jesus literally, physically became the Way. His death on our behalf provided the bridge to cross the chasm. It made possible our reconciliation with the Father.

There are those who resent the exclusiveness Jesus implies: "No one comes . . . except through me." "God isn't being fair," they say. "There must be another way for those who mean well and try hard, but haven't encountered *the* Way." If that were true, if there had been any other way, then the Father God's act of sending his dearly beloved Son to shoulder the world's sin as he died on the cross was the most hideously absurd act ever committed.

Unlike the sign on Mount Fuji, Jesus' message, "I am the Way," is clear and can be read by all. But the consequence of taking a wrong way, even with the best of intentions, is certain death.

The Way is not always smoothly paved. Following the Way is not always easy. It is not always fun. It does not always follow the most scenic route. Sometimes our feet will hurt; sometimes we will be bone-tired. Sometimes we will be lonely. At other times, the rudeness of other travelers along the way will irritate us. Sometimes we will wish we could turn back; we may even wonder at times if we have made a mistake.

But the Way is sure and leads to a sure end—eternal life through Jesus Christ, our Lord.

Jesus, our Way, we are hopelessly, helplessly lost without you. Give us direction today for the next step you would have us take.

9 | THE TRUTH

SCRIPTURE: PSALM 25:4–5, 8–9; JOHN 8:31–32

Jesus answered, "I am . . . *the truth* . . . No one comes to the
Father except through me."

JOHN 14:6

Jesus said, "If you hold to my teaching, you are really my
disciples. Then you will know *the truth*, and *the truth* will set
you free."

JOHN 8:31–32

Goaded by his fickle subjects, Pontius Pilate allowed the Truth to slip through his fingers, unnamed and unclaimed. He asked the right question, but he would not allow himself to see that the answer stood right before him.

Acknowledging the Truth would not have been politically expedient for Pontius Pilate. Indeed, pursuing truth can be costly, inconvenient, uncomfortable, and even dangerous. Many of us know people who have lost friends, jobs, material things, or their lives because they pursued truth.

But Pilate was mistaken if he really thought he could wash his hands of his responsibility to deal with the Truth (Matt. 27:24). Exposure to the Truth demands a response. For the One who said, "I am . . . the truth" went on to say, "No one comes to the Father except through me." By choosing the politically expedient way, Pilate lost his opportunity to find the Way and the Truth.

Truth is a searching spotlight, leaving no shadows in which to hide for those intent on pursuing evil. But for those seeking to follow God, this same spotlight is a welcome revealer of the obstacles over which they might otherwise have stumbled.

For us who would belong to God, following the Truth is not optional. The apostle Paul urges us to think on "whatsoever things are true" (Phil. 4:8 KJV). But like pure water and pure air around us, pure truth is hard to come by. The clarity of truth may be shadowed by unbelief, impure motives, and careless inattention. The impact of truth without love is like that of surgery on one whose body is incapable of healing. The impact of truth without wisdom is like that of light shining on the path of a blind person.

The beauty of Jesus, our Truth, is that he is the God of love as well as the God of wisdom. Jesus is God's true expression of himself.

Jesus Christ, our Truth, we worship you! Our falseness makes us squirm, but we know that we dare not, cannot hide. We confess that we have sinned. Realign us today next to the yardstick of your truth.

10   THE LIFE

Scripture: John 11:1–44

> I am . . . *the life*. No one comes to the Father except through me.
>
> John 14:6

> Jesus said to her, "I am the resurrection and *the life*. He who believes in me will live, even though he dies; and whoever lives and believes in me will never die."
>
> John 11:25–26

In the nine long months of waiting for a child to be born, we can see the ever-expanding belly—an indication of the new little life within it. We can feel, even sometimes see the baby's movements—surely this one will be a gymnast! And with the technology now available, we can hear our baby's heartbeat, watch movements in utero, know the gender, and learn much about this child for whom we wait. And wait.

Finally the day arrives, the newborn emerges, and the cord is clamped. Several seconds pass, each seeming like an eternity. Then we hear it, the first wail of this newborn baby! This is the cry that declares for all to hear, "I am breathing on my own. I am receiving the life you have hoped for, prayed for, and labored for." The gift of life demands a response.

The commencement of eternal life is also signaled by a birth, sometimes referred to as the second birth. Jesus told Nicodemus that "unless one is born anew, he cannot see the kingdom of God" (John 3:3 RSV). God himself, in the person of Jesus, has experienced indescribably excruciating labor to make our new birth possible. Others may have hoped and prayed for it to happen. Perhaps it is inevitable, but there must indeed come a time of affirmation, the baby's first wail: "Yes, I am receiving this life. Yes, I acknowledge the implications. I realize, as did the apostle Paul, that 'I have been crucified with Christ and I no longer live, but Christ lives in me'" (Gal. 2:20).

Naming Jesus *Life* gets at the very essence of what Christianity is all about. But in order to be Life for us, he first had to be our death. And because of who he was, God-man, his very real death could be followed by a very real coming alive, a resurrection.

Jesus felt pain at the death of his friend Lazarus. He wept. But the One who named himself both the Resurrection and the Life was able to lock this pain of death into that small sliver of eternity known as time.

Thou only art true Life,
To know Thee is to live
The more abundant life
That earth can never give:
O risen Lord! We live in Thee,
And Thou in us eternally.[2]

—E. Margaret Clarkson

Jesus Christ, because you first named yourself the Resurrection and the Life, we are able to call you by these names today. In doing so, we strain to catch a glimpse of what that abundant life, lived beyond time, will mean. Live through us today.

11 TEACHER

SCRIPTURE: PSALM 25:4–5, 8–9, 12; PSALM 31:8; PSALM 119:33; MATTHEW 5:2; JOHN 14:26

I will instruct you and teach you in the way you should go;
> I will counsel you and watch over you.

PSALM 32:8

And he will be called
> Wonderful Counselor.

ISAIAH 9:6

Rabbi, we know you are a *teacher* who has come from God.

JOHN 3:2

For the Holy Spirit will teach you.

LUKE 12:12

We have all been influenced by teachers. What qualities come to mind as we recall the best teachers we have known? May these qualities also be attributed to the greatest of all teachers, God himself?

A Teacher who will bend down and listen. What a gift we have in such a Teacher! The psalmist is confident that he will be heard, that God will "incline his ear" and hear what he has to say. "I have called upon thee, for thou wilt hear me, O God: incline thine ear unto me, and hear my speech" (Ps. 17:6 KJV).

A Teacher who knows his subject matter. Our Teacher is God himself. Who could better show us the Father and teach us his way? We are promised,

> When he, the Spirit of truth, comes, he will guide you into all truth. (John 16:13)

> But the Counselor, the Holy Spirit, whom the Father will send in my [Jesus'] name, will teach you all things. (John 14:26)

> [The Spirit] will not speak on his own; he will speak only what he hears . . . [He] will take from what is mine and make it known to you. (John 16:13, 15)

Indeed, our Teacher knows his subject matter.

A Teacher who knows his students. How well our Teacher knows us! "He lives with you and will be in you" (John 14:17). As the psalmist observed,

> O LORD, you have searched me
> and you know me.
> You know when I sit and when I rise;
> you perceive my thoughts from afar.

You discern my going out and my lying down,
  you are familiar with all my ways.
Before a word is on my tongue
  you know it completely, O LORD.

You hem me in—behind and before;
  you have laid your hand upon me. (Ps. 139:1–5)

It is both uncomfortable and comforting to be taught by One who knows us like this!

A Teacher who is able to individualize the instruction, who will challenge without becoming either frustrating or boring! The apostle Paul assures us that "God keeps faith, and he will not allow you to be tested above your powers, but when the test comes he will at the same time provide a way out, by enabling you to sustain it" (1 Cor. 10:13 NEB). Another student wrote:

How sweet are your words to my taste,
  sweeter than honey to my mouth!
I gain understanding from your precepts;
  therefore I hate every wrong path. (Ps. 119:103–104)

A Teacher who is an effective and ready counselor. The advice of our all-wise, all-knowing Teacher is the best and can be relied upon without hesitation. The prophet Isaiah called him Wonderful Counselor. (Isa. 9:6)

A Teacher who helps us meet our goals. We have a Teacher who wills for us to walk or "keep in step" (Gal. 5:25) with him. And we can be certain he will carry to completion the good work he has begun in our lives (Phil. 1:6).

Teacher, Counselor, Friend, how can we thank you? We are grateful that you receive the feeble attempts at thanks that we offer today and that you understand our hearts. May our thanks take the form of increased willingness to be shaped and taught by you and increased obedience to what you have already taught us.

12 THE ROOT, THE VINE, THE BRANCH, AND THE CUP

SCRIPTURE: JOHN 15:1–16

I, Jesus, have sent my angel to give you this testimony for the churches. I am *the Root* and the Offspring of David.

REVELATION 22:16

The Root of David has triumphed. He is able to open the scroll and its seven seals.

REVELATION 5:5

If some of the branches have been broken off, and you, though a wild olive shoot, have been grafted in among the others and now share in the nourishing sap from the olive root, do not boast over those branches. If you do, consider this: You do not support *the root*, but *the root* supports you.

ROMANS 11:17–18

I am the true *vine* . . . Remain in me, and I will remain in you. No branch can bear fruit by itself; it must remain in *the vine*.

JOHN 15:1, 4

I am *the vine*; you are the branches.

JOHN 15:5

Here is the man whose name is *the Branch*.

ZECHARIAH 6:12

A shoot will come up from the stump of Jesse;
    from his roots a *Branch* will bear fruit.
The Spirit of the LORD will rest on him—
    the Spirit of wisdom and of understanding.

ISAIAH 11:1–2

Then he took *the cup*, gave thanks and offered it to them,
saying, "Drink from it, all of you. This is my blood of the
covenant, which is poured out for many for the forgiveness
of sins."

MATTHEW 26:27–28

The Root, the Vine, the Branch, and the Cup: named in one sentence, they seem almost a contradiction! One might wish the writers of Scripture had consulted one another instead of muddling their metaphors. But on further reflection, these terms are neither contradictory nor muddled. All four point to what Jesus has done for us.

Unless it is planted in good soil, a vine will soon wither away. The soil in which this vine is planted is rich with the nutrients of the love of God. The apostle Paul prayed, "May your roots go down deep into the soil of God's marvelous love" (Eph. 3:17 TLB).

The root of the vine is not usually visible, but the life of the plant depends on it. It is through the root, firmly fixed in the soil, that moisture and nutrients are drawn into the rest of the plant. The deeper into the soil the root goes, the better able the plant is to bear fruit in times of drought. Deep roots make the plant less likely to break in a storm or high wind.

The plant springs up through the soil from the root. Jesus could therefore truly be the Root of David, since he was David's Creator as well as David's offspring or Branch. The rest of the plant does not support the root, but the root is the support system for the rest of the plant (Rom. 11:18). Jesus is truly our support system.

Jesus also named himself the Vine. It is to the vine that the branches must be directly connected, or they will die. After they are brought up through the root, nutrients and moisture are then brought to the branches through the vine. For a branch to be in close proximity to the vine is not enough—just as attending a church or being in a family where others are believers is not enough. The branches must belong to the plant itself. Jesus, the Vine, is our source of living water and nourishment.

Jesus is "the man whose name is the Branch" (Zech. 6:12). Jesse's tree, the once powerful kingdom of Israel, has been cut down, and compared to what it once was, only a stump is left (Isa. 11:1). But from this stump grows a living Branch, Jesus Christ himself. The purpose of the branch is to bear fruit. The fruit given by the man whose name is the Branch had a very special function.

At the last supper Jesus had with his disciples before he died, he took a cup filled with wine—fruit of the vine—and gave it to them. "Drink from it, all of you. This is my blood of the covenant, which is poured out for many for the forgiveness of sins" (Matt. 26:27–28).

Jesus—the Branch, the Vine, and the Root, springing from the soil of God's love—produced fruit that he poured out on our behalf!

Jesus Christ! You are all we need. We love you. Help us, your fellow branches, to bear fruit as we partake of the life of the Vine.

┊|13 ETERNAL GOD

SCRIPTURE: DEUTERONOMY 33:26–29; ROMANS 1:20

The *eternal God* is your refuge,
> and underneath are the everlasting arms.

DEUTERONOMY 33:27

Now to the King eternal, immortal, invisible, the only God, be
honor and glory for ever and ever. Amen.

1 TIMOTHY 1:17

Fettered by time as we are, it is hard for us to imagine what the word *eternal* means. People are born and they die. We light a match to start a fire, and when the wood is consumed, it extinguishes itself. Tasks are begun and they are completed. A day begins with the sun's apparent rising and ends when the sun appears to set. We hang a new calendar on the wall when a year begins and take it down when a year ends. What is it never to have begun and never to end? Who is the eternal God? What does eternity mean, anyway?

A simple math problem brings to mind one picture of eternity: the problem is to divide three into one. Now, there is a long math problem! Infinitely, eternally long! In fact, if someone starts to work that problem today, it will never be completed, even if that person keeps working through all eternity! Our mathematicians will simply have to decide when to go on to other things. For no matter how many times the three is divided into the one, the one is never completely used up.

The eternal One who is our God has made all his resources available for us to draw on. Even when we are released from the bondage of time, we can keep drawing from the eternal One strength, grace, wisdom, and all that we need throughout all of eternity. The supply will never be exhausted.

Infinite, Eternal One! Unwittingly we limit you with our finity and shortsightedness. Help us to see more clearly what it means to draw on your infinite, eternal resources. We entrust the time you have given us today back to you, mindful that our times are truly in your hands. And you have made a way for us to share eternity with you. Receive our deep gratitude this day, Father of Eternity, Infinite, Eternal One!

14 | THE MORNING STAR

Scripture: John 1:4–9; 3:19–21

> I, Jesus, have sent my angel to give you this testimony for the churches. I am . . . the bright *Morning Star*.
>
> REVELATION 22:16

> To him who overcomes and does my will to the end, I will give authority over the nations. . . . I will also give him the *morning star*.
>
> REVELATION 2:26, 28

> I see him, but not now;
>   I behold him, but not near.
> A star will come out of Jacob;
>   a scepter will rise out of Israel.
>
> NUMBERS 24:17

*W*hat is a star? Stars are not the mysteries they once were. Thanks to modern science, we can understand their composition, how far away they are, and how large they are with much more clarity than did our ancestors.

What is a star? A star is a source of light. That light comes from the burning up of its very essence. It is not reflected light, such as comes to us from the moon and planets.

Perhaps understanding these two types of light can help us to understand Jesus' two seemingly paradoxical statements, "I am the light of the world" and "you are the light of the world." Like a bright and burning ball of fire, Jesus is our source of light. As we reflect his light, we, too, can be light to our world.

To be light, a light source must spend itself. It must literally use itself up. It is difficult for us to fathom what that means for a star, because the "using up" takes place over millions or perhaps billions of years. But consider a burning candle.* Even as we watch it give light for us, we can see that the candle is being used up, spent.

How like our Lord! In order to be light for us, he literally spent himself.

O Splendor of God's glory bright,
   From light eternal bringing light,
Thou Light of light, light's living Spring
   True Day, all days illumining;

Come, very Sun of heaven's love,
   In lasting radiance from above,

---

* If you are using this meditation with a group, you might like to have a candle burning while you talk.

And pour the Holy Spirit's ray
On all we think or do today.

Dawn's glory gilds the earth and skies,
Let him, our perfect Morn, arise,
The Word in God the Father one,
The Father imaged in the Son.

—AMBROSE OF MILAN (340–397)

Jesus, our bright Morning Star! Forgive us for taking for granted what it cost you to be light for us.

Jesus, our bright Morning Star! Help us this day to be clearer reflectors of your light, so that we, too, may "shine like stars in the universe as [we] hold out the word of life" (Phil. 2:15–16).

$\S$ | 15   ROCK

SCRIPTURE: MATTHEW 7:24–27; EPHESIANS 2:19–22;
      1 PETER 2:6–8

I love you, O LORD, my strength.

The LORD is my *rock*, my fortress and my deliverer;
    my God is my *rock*, in whom I take refuge.
    He is my shield and the horn of my salvation, my stronghold. . . .

For who is God besides the LORD?
    And who is the *Rock* except our God? . . .

The LORD lives! Praise be to my *Rock*!
    Exalted be God my Savior!

PSALM 18:1–2, 31, 46

He lifted me out of the slimy pit,
    out of the mud and mire;
he set my feet on a *rock*
    and gave me a firm place to stand.

PSALM 40:2

*H*ave you ever considered how truly desperate Jacob must have been to choose a rock for a pillow? A rock is hardly a comfortable place to sit for a long time, let alone to sleep on all night. A prolonged or abrupt encounter with a rock is not what most of us would consider comfortable—it can indeed be downright painful!

But there is a big difference between comfortable and comforting. A rock is a secure place on which to build. Unlike the house built on shifting sand, the house built on the rock withstood the ravages of rain and flood (Matt. 7:24).

A rock is a safe place on which to stand after one has been slipping and sliding about in quicksand (Ps. 40:2). A large rock is secure, fixed, and unmovable. It represents constancy and permanence, something to grab hold of when everything else about us seems to be changing.

A rock can be a shelter under which to take refuge. It can provide shade from a merciless sun or spare one from the fury of a driving rain.

An abrupt encounter with a rock cannot be ignored. We cannot pretend it isn't there, especially if the encounter has been painful. Jacob slept with a rock for a pillow. He dreamed and afterward awoke with an awareness of the presence of the Lord. He made a solemn vow as his response (Gen. 28:10–22). In the parable of the tenants (Mark 12:1–12), the visit of the owner's beloved son could not be ignored. The response of the tenants was to reject and kill the owner's son. As Jesus concluded his parable, he quoted Scripture:

The stone the builders rejected
    has become the capstone;
the Lord has done this,
    and it is marvelous in our eyes. (Mark 12:10–11)

The same stone will be tripped over by some and used as a firm place to stand by others (Isa. 8:14; 28:16).

Jesus Christ is my Rock. He is my refuge, my foundation, my resting place, and my security in the midst of turmoil. The reality of who he is and what he has done looms large in front of me and cannot be ignored. Today my encounter with the Rock demands a response:

Lord, God, "may the words of my mouth and the meditation of my heart be pleasing in your sight," O Lord, my Rock and my Redeemer. (Ps. 19:14)

$\frac{3}{6}$ | 16   HOLY SPIRIT

SCRIPTURE: JOHN 14:15–27

And the *Spirit* of God was hovering over the waters.

GENESIS 1:2

God is spirit, and his worshipers must worship in spirit and in truth.

JOHN 4:24

But the Counselor, the *Holy Spirit*, whom the Father will send in my [Jesus'] name, will teach you all things and will remind you of everything I have said to you.

JOHN 14:26

Don't you know that you yourselves are God's temple and that God's *Spirit* lives in you?

1 CORINTHIANS 3:16

We do not know what we ought to pray for, but the *Spirit* himself intercedes for us with groans that words cannot express. And he who searches our hearts knows the mind of the *Spirit*, because the *Spirit* intercedes for the saints in accordance with God's will.

ROMANS 8:26–27

Where can I go from your *Spirit*?

    Where can I flee from your presence?

If I go up to the heavens, you are there;

    if I make my bed in the depths, you are there.

Psalm 139:7–8

*S*ome of us can remember attempting to make an international telephone call before the days of electronic mail, iPods and iPhones, instant messaging, and communications satellites. We marvel at the ease and efficiency of today's global communication. But with the best of our information technology, there are sometimes power outages and other times when our equipment fails us. Sometimes we receive no response. Sometimes we receive a busy signal or a recording inviting us to leave a name and number after the "beep."

As wonderful as satellite telecommunication is, it doesn't begin to compare with the communication system available for an earth-child with her heavenly Father.

A four-year-old girl asked, "Can God really hear everyone who is praying?"

"Yes, he can," she was told.

"Even if a lot of people all over the world are praying at once?"

"He hears them all," was the reply.

"God must wear an awfully big shirt," reflected the child, after a pause.

Even we who are older than four are full of wonder as we think about prayer. It is because God is Spirit, and not bound to a shirt of any size, that prayer is possible. Because God is Spirit, God is always there, the line is never busy, we never get a recording, and we never have to wait.

Often we don't know what to say or what to ask or even how to ask. God, the Holy Spirit, conveys the message that we would have given if we could.

Because God is Spirit, God can be simultaneously with us and with people who are dear to us but far away. We have a link to our distant loved ones that those without God, the Spirit, cannot comprehend.

Because God is Spirit, there isn't any place we can go where God is not. It would be futile to try to hide or to run away.

Because of the function of God the Spirit, this is not the person of the Godhead that many of us focus on in our prayers and thoughts of God. When we look through a clear, clean window, we don't usually think about the window. We tend to focus on, and think about, what we see through the window. The Holy Spirit is much like that window. Because the Spirit is there, we are able to see the Father and the Son. How much and how clearly would we see if the window weren't there?

Come, O Creator Spirit blest,
And in our hearts take up thy rest;
Spirit of grace with heavenly aid
Come to the souls whom thou hast made.
Show us the Father, Holy One,
Help us to know th' Eternal Son;
Spirit Divine, for evermore
Thee will we trust and thee adore.

—Anonymous, tenth century (Latin)
Trans. George Rawson (1807–1889)

O, Holy Spirit, breath of God! You are the great Communicator and Illuminator. We worship you today.

17 LIVING WATER

Come, all you who are thirsty,
    come to the waters;
and you who have no money,
    come.

ISAIAH 55:1

Then Jesus declared, "He who believes in me will never be thirsty."

JOHN 6:35

Wash me, and I will be whiter than snow.

PSALM 51:7

When you pass through the waters,
    I will be with you;
and when you pass through the rivers,
    they will not sweep over you.

ISAIAH 43:2

Jesus answered her, "If you knew the gift of God and who it is that asks you for a drink, you would have asked him and he would have given you *living water*."

JOHN 4:10

*W*e might value water more if we had to carry it in jars from the edge of town, bearing on our shoulders all the water our household needed each day! But even we who take our abundant water supply for granted can attest to the fact that after several hours of physical exertion on a hot day, nothing quenches thirst like a glass of cold water, no matter what the soft drink advertisers would have us think.

Another luxury that not all peoples of all cultures have been able to enjoy is that of frequent bathing—the opportunity to become clean! What a gift it is to be able to wash.

How vital water is for all that grows on the earth—trees, plants, flowers, grass, fruits, vegetables, grains, and all creatures. They all would die if it were not for water.

> The rain and the snow
>   come down from heaven,
> and do not return to it
>   without watering the earth
> and making it bud and flourish,
>   so that it yields seed for the sower and bread for the eater.
>   (Isa. 55:10)

And consider the power of moving water. It alters and erodes riverbanks and shorelines. Sometimes the energy from falling water has been harnessed to provide electricity for entire communities.

Buoyancy—we are sometimes inclined to forget this property of water. Good swimming instructors frequently tell their students: "Swim *through* the water; don't struggle so hard to get above it. The water itself will hold you up if you let it."

Where water is abundant, people have found ways to transport themselves and their goods through it. And children of all ages have enjoyed playing in water.

Sometimes we have gone about thirsty, dirty, parched, and powerless. God has put Living Water at our disposal, but we have sat beside our empty pails, either ignorant or afraid of the implications of Living Water. We can identify with Jill, a character in one of C. S. Lewis's Chronicles of Narnia:

> "Are you not thirsty?" said the Lion.
>
> "I'm dying of thirst," said Jill.
>
> "Then drink," said the Lion.
>
> "May I—could I—would you mind going away while I do?" said Jill.
>
> The Lion answered this only by a look and a very low growl . . .
>
> "I daren't come and drink," said Jill.
>
> "Then you will die of thirst," said the Lion.
>
> "O dear!" said Jill, coming another step nearer. "I suppose I must go and look for another stream then."
>
> "There is no other stream," said the Lion.[3]

Jesus, our Living Water, forgive us. We have fought and struggled, trying to hold ourselves up in our own strength. We fail to appropriate the fact that as we rest in you, our Living Water, you are with us and are holding us up. Thank you that you yourself are what we need, and all we need, to quench our souls' thirst. We are grateful for the cleansing that you alone can provide us. We are awed at the power available to us. "The Lord is our strength and song. He is become our salvation. Today with joy, we will draw water from the wells of salvation." (Isa. 12:2–3, paraphrase) Receive our thanks this day.

18 THE GENTLE WHISPER

SCRIPTURE: 1 KINGS 19:9–18; 1 SAMUEL 3:2–10

> The LORD said, "Go out and stand on the mountain . . . for the LORD is about to pass by." . . . And after the fire came a *gentle whisper.*
>
> 1 KINGS 19:11–12

*E*nter: one of God's faithful servants. God has only recently used him in a mighty and powerful way. But now this servant of the Lord is feeling alone, discouraged, and afraid.

The message comes: "Go out and stand on the mountain in the presence of the LORD, for the LORD is about to pass by" (1 Kings 19:11).

What must God's servant have felt and thought? Perhaps some skepticism. Surely some amazement. What will it sound like when the mighty Yahweh, Creator of the universe—the One who had poured fire from heaven to consume the water-drenched sacrifice offered by his servant—passes by?

Act I: A great and powerful wind rages and roars, tearing mountains apart and splitting huge rocks in two. Is the Lord God in the howling of the wind?*

---

* If you are using this with a group, you can provide a few simple sound effects. (Hide objects behind the podium or in a paper grocery sack. For rocks breaking in the wind, hit two wooden blocks together. For the earthquake, place several wooden blocks in a shoe box and shake box from side to side. For fire, wrinkle a piece of wax paper.

Act II: Rumble, rumble! The earth itself, once so firm and solid, now begins to shake and tremble. To the helpless and uncertain onlooker, even seconds seem like eternities. Is God speaking in the midst of the earth's rumbles?

Act III: Hear now a crackling, spitting fire, blazing and consuming all in its path. Is this the sound of the Lord God passing by?

Act IV: In a dramatic contrast to what has just transpired, a peaceful stillness settles over the scene. Listen! Do you hear the gentle whisper? *The Lord God is passing by!* His servant hears and is encouraged.

O God, our Father, sometimes the clamor with which we are surrounded all but drowns out your gentle whisper. Help us to become better listeners. We would claim the prayer of the child Samuel: "Speak, for your servant is listening" (1 Sam. 3:10).

19 LAST ADAM

Scripture: Genesis 2:7; Genesis 3;
1 Corinthians 15:20–25, 45–47

> The Lord God formed the man from the dust of the ground
> and breathed into his nostrils the breath of life, and the man
> became a living being.
>
> Genesis 2:7

> For as in Adam all die, so in Christ all will be made alive.
>
> 1 Corinthians 15:22

> So it is written: "The first man Adam became a living being;"
> the *last Adam*, a life-giving spirit.
>
> 1 Corinthians 15:45

It had been an adam* who introduced sin into the world.
An adam cut the chasm that separated the holy God
from the creatures who were his image bearers.

So it had to be an adam, a son of Adam, who would build
the bridge to cross that chasm of eternal death. And it had to be
an adam who was perfect and without sin. We cannot fully comprehend what had to happen. God himself became Adam. The
eternal God became a human embryo and locked himself inside

---

* *Adam* is the Hebrew word for "man" and may be derived from *adamah*, the Hebrew
for "ground."

NAMES OF GOD

a woman's uterus for nine months. He was born in a barn, and his first bed was a box full of animal feed.

The infant "last Adam" must surely have cried when he was hungry or wet.

As an adult, the last Adam wept when his good friend, Lazarus, died.

After one exhausting day, he fell asleep in the boat of his fishermen friends.

He was so furious that a place of worship had been desecrated and corrupted that he made a whip and literally drove away those who were responsible.

He enjoyed relaxing at the home of his friends, Mary, Martha, and Lazarus.

The devil himself tried every one of his tricks on the last Adam, attempting in vain to find a vulnerable area.

The last Adam submitted to the most humiliating of deaths—as a criminal, on a cross. He experienced something no other adam needs to experience—total separation from the Father God.

All praise to thee, Eternal Lord,
Clothed in a garb of flesh and blood;
Choosing a manger for thy throne,
While worlds on worlds are thine alone.

—MARTIN LUTHER, 1524

Accept our worship, eternal Lord, you who became for us the last Adam.

20 REDEEMER

SCRIPTURE: JOB 19:25–27; ISAIAH 44:6–8

Our *Redeemer*—the LORD Almighty is his name—
> is the Holy One of Israel.

ISAIAH 47:4

I know that my *Redeemer* lives,
> and that in the end he will stand upon the earth.

JOB 19:25

There is a story that some of us heard as children. A young boy made for himself a beautiful little sailboat, sanding, painting, and gluing each of its parts with great care. It became his favorite possession, and almost daily he went to sail it on the river near his home. One day a storm came up suddenly, the string on the boat broke, and the boat got away from him. He spent many days searching for the boat along the banks of the river, and he began to fear that he would never see it again.

Months later, his grandfather took him to town, and as they were poking around in a secondhand shop, the boy spotted a familiar-looking boat, high on one of the shelves, with a price tag attached to it.

"Let me see that boat," he cried. "I think that's the boat I made."

The shopkeeper obligingly took the boat from the shelf.

"See! These are my initials! I carved them in the bottom! This is my boat."

"I'm sorry, son. I bought that boat from the man who brought it into the shop. If you want the boat, you'll have to pay for it."

Sadly the boy left the shop. For the next few weeks he worked hard doing every odd job anyone would give him, carefully saving every penny.

At last he had the required amount of money. He went back to the shop and redeemed for himself the boat he had made.

The seeming injustice of having to pay for something that was one's own in the first place rankles a little. But that is the essence of what it means to redeem.

Christ our Creator made us and stamped us with his own image. Then we became separated from him.

Christ our Redeemer bought back the right to own us by paying a price so awful we cannot comprehend it.

> I will sing of my Redeemer
> And his wondrous love to me;
> On the cruel cross he suffered
> From the curse to set me free.
>
> Sing, oh sing, of my Redeemer
> With his blood he purchased me.

On the cross he sealed my pardon,
Paid the debt and made me free.

—Philip P. Bliss

Creator, Redeemer God, you have twice the right to own us. You hold our purchase agreement, signed in your blood. Yet some of us, fools that we are, keep trying to snatch back ownership for ourselves.

Give us just a glimpse, today, of what it cost you to redeem us. Receive our bodies as living sacrifices. Receive the words of our mouths and the thoughts of our hearts.

21 MERCIFUL GOD

SCRIPTURE: EXODUS 25:10–22; EPHESIANS 2:1–5

"I am *merciful*," declares the LORD,
    "I will not be angry forever."

JEREMIAH 3:12

Your Father is *merciful*.

LUKE 6:36

God, have mercy on me, a sinner.

LUKE 18:13

But because of his great love for us, God, who is rich in
mercy, made us alive with Christ even when we were dead in
transgressions—it is by grace you have been saved.

EPHESIANS 2:4–5

I will sing of the mercies of the LORD for ever: with my mouth
will I make known thy faithfulness to all generations.

PSALM 89:1 KJV

For God's mercy to hold any meaning for us, we must first begin to understand the intensity of God's holiness and the immensity of our sin. The depth of mercy is in direct relation to the gravity of the wrong.

Sometimes we think of mercy as a rug under which to scoot dirt, or as a frosting to fill and cover that section of the cake that fell. But mercy is more than the superficial covering or over-looking of a wrong. Such a notion makes a mockery of God's holiness. Mercy deals with the wrong itself.

In the book of Exodus, we have recorded for us the careful and detailed instructions God gave the Israelites for building the tabernacle. This was to be their place of worship. In the taber-nacle was to be the ark of the covenant, which represented the presence of the holy God. The ark was to be a box, covered inside and out with gold. The box was to be made with two rings on each side, through which gold-covered poles were to be placed. No one, under any circumstance, was to touch the ark itself. In it were placed the tablets on which were inscribed the Ten Commandments, representing the law of God. A gold cover with two cherubim "of hammered gold" (Ex. 25:18) was placed on top of the ark. This cover has sometimes been called the mercy seat. The ark with this covering was placed behind a curtain. Only the high priest was allowed to enter that Most Holy Place—and he only once a year on the Day of Atonement. The Israelites had before them a promise that God's mercy would cover God's law, which they were unable to keep. They could partake of that mercy, but since the wrong had not yet been made right, their participation had to be from a distance.

At the moment of Jesus' death, the curtain, which for so many years had separated the ark and its mercy seat from view, was ripped from top to bottom. Justice had been done. God himself had paid dearly to right sin's wrongs. The torn curtain stated dramatically that now God's mercy could be available to all who would receive it. Now his mercy was accessible in a way it never had been before.

> Let us wonder,
> > grace and justice join,
> > and point to mercy's store;
> When through grace in Christ our trust is,
> Justice smiles and asks no more.
> He who washed us with his blood,
> Has secured our way to God.
>
> Let us praise and join the chorus
> Of the saints enthroned on high;
> Here they trusted him before us,
> Now their praises fill the sky:
> "Thou hast washed us with thy blood;
> Thou art worthy, Lamb of God!" Amen.
>
> —JOHN NEWTON, 1774

Merciful God, we confess before you that we have sinned, even this very day. You have not ignored our sin, even though we have a tendency to do so. You have not glossed over it, even though we try to do that as well. You have paid dearly that we might receive mercy instead of the justice we deserve. With gratitude we clothe ourselves in your righteousness today.

⟨⟩ | 22 LIKE AN EAGLE

SCRIPTURE: DEUTERONOMY 32:9–14; EXODUS 19:4;
ISAIAH 40:28–31

[The Lord] shielded him and cared for him;
    he guarded him as the apple of his eye,
like an eagle that stirs up its nest
    and hovers over its young,
that spreads its wings to catch them
    and carries them on its pinions.
The LORD alone led him.

DEUTERONOMY 32:10–12

You yourselves have seen what I did to Egypt, and how I
carried you on eagles' wings and brought you to myself.

EXODUS 19:4

But those who hope in the LORD
    will renew their strength.
They will soar on wings like eagles.

ISAIAH 40:31

*T*he eagle is one of the largest and most powerful birds in the world. Some eagles weigh as much as twelve or thirteen pounds and have a wingspan of about seven feet.

The nests of eagles are called eyries. They are built mainly of sticks and are often lined with fresh green leaves while they are being used. Once a year the female lays one or two eggs, and they are carefully tended, sometimes even by the male eagle, until they hatch in about forty days. Both parents then guard the nest and take food to their young.

At about eleven or twelve weeks, a curious thing happens. If the eaglets have not yet ventured forth on their own, the parent eagle "stirs" or rocks the nest, tipping the eaglets out! The young eaglets flap about in panic, still novices at this flying business. The parent eagle hovers watchfully, waiting for the critical moment. With wings spread wide, the eagle then swoops down underneath those babies and delivers them back to the security of the eyrie.

Ours is a God of powerful gentleness. Ours is a God whose timing is perfect. Like the parent eagle, God is sensitive to our needs. God knows when the nest has become too comfortable and needs a little stirring. He, too, watches carefully and, as with spread wings, catches us up, bringing us to himself. But he wants us to learn from our fluttering and flapping. He wants us to leave behind our panic and to learn to wait on him. Then, with our eyes on our parent eagle, we will begin to know what it means to soar on eagle's wings!

Today we praise you, O God, for eagle's wings that keep us safe, help us soar, and bring us to yourself.

23 | AUTHOR AND EDITOR

SCRIPTURE: EPHESIANS 1:3–10; 2:10

> Let us fix our eyes on Jesus, the *author and [editor*]* of our faith.
>
> HEBREWS 12:2, PARAPHRASE

*T*here isn't a human author who doesn't, or wouldn't, benefit from a good editor. The author conceives and births the idea, but a second pair of eyes sees it in a different way and with a fresh perspective.

A case can also be made for the idea that human editors—those who perfect, polish, and apply the finishing touches, those who see the work through to completion—need authors.

As our Author, Jesus Christ conceived the very idea of us before the foundation of the world. He made possible both our birth and our new birth.

But he hasn't stopped there. He has the will, the ability, and the authority to see us—his workmanship, his poem (Eph. 2:10)—through to completion. Paul tells the Philippians that he

---

* The Greek has been translated "finisher" (KJV) and "perfecter" (RSV, NIV, and Ryrie). My rendering, "editor," has much the same connotation.

NAMES OF GOD

is confident that "he who began a good work in you will carry it on to completion until the day of Christ Jesus" (Phil. 1:6).

Sometimes we question or chafe at all the editing that is prescribed for us. But ours is not an Editor capable of error or capriciousness. Unlikely as it may seem at times, we will someday be all that we are meant to be: Jesus' masterpiece.

Lord Jesus, today we thank you that you who authored us have not given up on your work in progress. Remain with us, we pray, until we are complete in you, a poem that brings you praise!

24 | THE GREAT SHEPHERD

SCRIPTURE: PSALM 23; MATTHEW 18:12–14; JOHN 10:1–8; HEBREWS 13:20–21

Our Lord Jesus, that *great Shepherd* of the sheep . . .

HEBREWS 13:20

I am the good shepherd; I know my sheep and my sheep know me—just as the Father knows me and I know the Father—and I lay down my life for the sheep.

JOHN 10:14–15

 good shepherd, or pastor, must have a combination of almost paradoxical qualities.

We who are not shepherds tend to think of a pastoral scene as being peaceful and quiet. The picture is full of lush greens, blue sky, and a crystal-clear pool of water. No sounds more harsh than those of chirping birds can be heard. Our image of the shepherd tends to be that of a person both gentle and patient. The good shepherd thoughtfully provides the best nourishment and care possible for his sheep. He is willing to risk personal hardship and danger for them. With the picture as sketched so far, we like thinking of ourselves as sheep under the watch of such a shepherd!

But sheep are stupid creatures. Often they don't have the sense to follow the shepherd, and he must nudge or even push them from behind or alongside. Sheep are willful creatures, often straying, searching for something better, somewhere else.

The good shepherd knows each one of his sheep by name, and each is important to him. He will leave the rest of the flock to search for one that wanders off. The good shepherd persistently combs the countryside until he locates the missing sheep.

Here the pastoral picture changes. The once blue sky darkens with an approaching storm. The sheep is caught in a thorn bush at the brink of a precipice. The good shepherd has to act swiftly, forcefully. He places his shepherd's crook firmly around the neck of his sheep. Holding aside some of the thorny branches with one arm, the shepherd pulls—yes, yanks—his sheep free from the bush, bringing some of the thorns and smaller branches with it.

Having found shelter, the good shepherd has to pull out the thorns, one by one, as his sheep bleats in pain.

On the way home, the shepherd has to kill a wild animal that would otherwise have attacked. The sheep trembles and is afraid.

The good shepherd is indeed gentle and patient, a loving provider of care and nourishment. He is also strong and able and will push or pull hard when love for his sheep dictates that he do so.

The God of love my Shepherd is,
And he that doth me feed:
While He is mine and I am His,
What can I want or need?

He leads me to the tender grass
Where I both feed and rest;
Then to the streams that gently pass,
In both I have the best.

Or if I stray, He doth convert,
And bring my mind in frame:
And all this not for my desert,
But for His holy name.

—George Herbert (based on Psalm 23)

Great and Good Shepherd, we marvel that you know each of us by name and that you go out of your way to find us when we wander off. You provide for us with great care. We are grateful that you lead us, even sometimes carry us, through the dark and sharowy places. Lead us safely home, we pray.

25   LAMB

SCRIPTURE: JOHN 1:29–34; REVELATION 5:12;
1 CORINTHIANS 5:7–8

Abraham answered, "God himself will provide the *lamb* for
the burnt offering, my son."

GENESIS 22:8

Tell the whole community of Israel that on the tenth day of
this month each man is to take a *lamb* for his family, one for
each household.

EXODUS 12:3

He was led like a *lamb* to the slaughter,
     and as a sheep before her shearers is silent,
     so he did not open his mouth.

ISAIAH 53:7

The next day John saw Jesus coming toward him and said,
"Look, the *Lamb* of God, who takes away the sin of the world!"

JOHN 1:29

[You were redeemed] with the precious blood of Christ, a *lamb*
without blemish or defect.

1 PETER 1:19

Then I saw a *Lamb*, looking as if it had been slain, standing in the center of the throne, encircled by the four living creatures and the elders. . . .

In a loud voice they sang:

> "Worthy is the *Lamb*, who was slain,
> to receive power and wealth and wisdom and strength
> and honor and glory and praise!"

REVELATION 5:6, 12

They have washed their robes and made them white in the blood of the *Lamb*. . . . For the *Lamb* at the center of the throne will be their shepherd.

REVELATION 7:14, 17

Can it be that the Creator of all the galaxies was also named the Lamb? The gentle creature of whom the poet asked:

> Little lamb, who made thee?
> Dost thou know who made thee?
> Gave thee life, and bid thee feed
> By the stream and o'er the mead,
> Gave thee clothing of delight,
> Softest clothing, woolly, bright;
> Gave thee such a tender voice,
> Making all the vales rejoice?

Little lamb, who made thee?
Dost thou know who made thee?
Little lamb, I'll tell thee,
Little lamb, I'll tell thee.
He is called by thy name,
For He calls Himself a Lamb.
He is meek, and He is mild,
He became a little child.
I a child, and thou a lamb,
We are called by His name.
Little lamb, God bless thee!
Little lamb, God bless thee!

—WILLIAM BLAKE, *Songs of Innocence*

The lamb, even today, symbolizes innocence and purity. Only a pure unblemished lamb could be a sacrifice. A spotted lamb was not acceptable. The sacrificial lamb could not have any flaw or deformity. It could not harbor a parasite or suffer from any ailment. It had to be the firstborn of its mother.

The offering of a lamb had to be from an obedient heart in order to be acceptable. This was true of the very first offering mentioned in Scripture—Abel's offering of a lamb from his flock (Gen. 4)—and continues to be true for every offering thereafter. King Saul's proposed offering was rejected because he had been disobedient (1 Sam. 15). He was told, "To obey is better than sacrifice, and to heed is better than the fat of rams" (v.

22). The offering of the Lamb was an offering of obedience. The writer of Hebrews says of Christ, the Lamb, "Although he was a son, he learned obedience from what he suffered" (5:8).

For the offering to be complete, the blood of the Lamb had to be shed. "And without the shedding of blood there is no forgiveness" (Heb 9:22).

All the animals sacrificed in the time of the Old Testament were object lessons, pointing toward the one sufficient, worthy sacrifice. Because all of us have sinned, the only One who could provide an acceptable sacrifice was God himself. Abraham was more right than he knew when he told Isaac, "God himself will provide the lamb for the burnt offering" (Gen. 22:8).

God's Lamb, holy, pure, perfect, and altogether worthy, shed his blood as an offering to atone for our sins. For us, the Creator of the galaxies became a Child, who became the Lamb of God.

The wonder is that "we are called by His name"! What does it mean for me, today, that I am called a lamb? What does it mean for me, today, that Jesus is the Lamb?

> "Worthy is the Lamb, who was slain,
> to receive power and wealth and wisdom
> and strength and honor and glory and praise!" (Rev. 5:12)

Worthy Lamb of God, receive our praise and gratitude today for your great sacrifice on our behalf.

§|26 IMMANUEL— GOD WITH US

Scripture: Matthew 1:18–25

> The virgin will be with child and will give birth to a son, and they will call him *Immanuel*—which means, "God with us."
>
> Matthew 1:23

*I*mmanuel *means a restored relationship.* When sin entered the world, there was a real sense in which the holy God was prevented from being with the men and women he had created. The God-man had to come in order to bring about a reconciliation. It is because of the death and resurrection of the Immanuel that we can know that God is with us.

Immanuel means there is One who knows how we feel, who identifies with us. Sometimes God gives us a hint of his kind of empathy through another person. For example, a young mother had ventured out to the grocery store with her three small children. It was her first such trip after the birth of her third baby. As she approached the checkout lanes, the three-year-old managed to knock a large jar of grape jelly onto the floor, leaving in her wake a huge puddle of broken glass and gooey grape jelly. The five-year-old announced in no uncertain terms that she *had* to go to the bathroom, *now.* The baby's wails announced loudly to the entire store that he was hungry. Every checkout lane had a long line of shoppers with heavily laden carts. A woman at the head of one of the lanes steered the young mother in front of her.

"You go first," she said. "I have five children of my own, and I know how you feel."

Immanuel means we don't have to feel alone. There is often an aloneness that comes even in the midst of a large crowd of people—just ask any young child who has ever been lost in such a crowd. There is the aloneness of being misunderstood. There is the aloneness of being in an empty house or apartment, all by oneself, night after night. And there is the aloneness of trying to carry a heavy load without help.

God With Us, your promise, first offered in the darkest of times, gave hope. And you are still with us in our darkest times. Our hearts are grateful to you, Immanuel.

27   POTTER

SCRIPTURE: ISAIAH 64:8; JEREMIAH 18:6; ROMANS 9:21;
EPHESIANS 2:10; 2 CORINTHIANS 4:7

You are the *potter*;
we are all the work of your hand.

ISAIAH 64:8

"O house of Israel, can I not do with you as this *potter* does?"
declares the LORD. "Like clay in the hand of the *potter*, so are
you in my hand."

JEREMIAH 18:6

uch! I don't like the way you're pressing and squeezing
me! . . .

That's to work the air bubbles out, you say? So I won't crack
later on? Oh . . .

You wouldn't throw me on that moving wheel, would you?
It's spinning so fast; I'm not ready for anything like that yet . . .

But you're ready? And that's all that matters? Hmmm . . .

Hey! This hurts! Don't you think about my feelings at all? . . .

Check out the scars in the Potter's hands . . . What kind of an
answer is that anyway? . . .

I don't think I like being this shape. And while we're on that subject, the color of the glaze you've chosen for me isn't at all becoming, if you ask me . . .

You didn't ask me? Oh . . .

Surely you aren't going to make me just another ordinary water pot, are you? I had so hoped to be something unique—a priceless *objet d'art* . . .

Wait a minute! You weren't planning to put me in the kiln, were you? It's hot in there! Why, if I do get out of that oven, I won't ever be the same again! . . .

That was your plan, you say? To make me strong and usable? A jar to hold living water? That the excellency of the power may be of God and not of . . . oh. I think I'm beginning to see.

> But who are you, a mere human being, to talk back to God? Shall what is formed say to the one who formed it, "Why did you make me like this?" Does not the potter have the right to make out of the same lump of clay some pottery for noble purposes and some for disposal of refuse? (Rom. 9:20–21 TNIV).

Have thine own way, Lord! Have thine own way!
Thou are the Potter; I am the clay.
Mold me and make me, after thy will,
While I am waiting, yielded and still.

—ADELAIDE A. POLLARD, 1902

28 ABBA, FATHER

SCRIPTURE: LUKE 15:11–31

You received the Spirit of sonship. And by him we cry, *"Abba, Father."* The Spirit himself testifies with our spirit that we are God's children. Now if we are children, then we are heirs— heirs of God and co-heirs with Christ.

ROMANS 8:15–17

This, then, is how you should pray:

> "Our *Father* in heaven,
> hallowed be your name."

MATTHEW 6:9

When Israel was a child, I loved him,
and out of Egypt I called my son. . . .
It was I who taught Ephraim to walk,
taking them by the arms.

HOSEA 11:1, 3

Be imitators of God, therefore, as dearly loved children.

EPHESIANS 5:1

*F*atherhood is initiated by the act of the father, not the child. No child can choose his own father. In the same way, our relationship with our heavenly Father exists because he took the initiative.

Fathers often have children who resemble them. That is how it should be with our heavenly Father. In human relationships, children may look like their fathers because they share some of the same genes and chromosomes. Our heavenly Father has created us in his own image. So we resemble him in a way his other creatures do not. In addition, little children watch their fathers and become like them by imitating them. Children learn to copy mannerisms, speech patterns, and other habits. They may try on a parent's shoes or clothing in order to be like the parent. They learn to value what the parent values. In much the same way, we who are God's children are to imitate him and to work at becoming children who resemble their Father.

A father is accessible to his child. A busy and important business executive has an outer office where secretaries screen his calls and where visitors wait. They may enter the inner office only after they are properly announced. But when the executive's young child arrives on the scene, the formalities are dispensed with. The child calls excitedly, "Daddy!" toddles in, and plops down on the father's lap. Our heavenly Father has made himself accessible to us. We need not wait to be announced or to have our credentials checked. He is always ready to hear us and to converse with us.

A father's child is usually his heir. The heir is the one who is legally entitled to receive what has belonged to the father. Think of all that belongs to our heavenly Father! Because of our relationship with him, we are entitled to receive it! As the apostle Paul put it, "Now if we are children, then we are heirs—heirs of God and co-heirs with Christ" (Rom. 8:17).

The father loves his child. There are human fathers who don't love their children. Sometimes God puts in our path the child of such a person, and we have the opportunity to love that child with a fatherlike love. Without a human example, such a child has a hard time seeing God as a Father. Some of us have been blessed with human fathers who do love us dearly. We have been given an object lesson, a hint of what being loved by the heavenly Father is like!

Our loving Father longs to teach us how to walk. "It was I who taught Ephraim to walk, taking them by the arms," writes the prophet Hosea of the Father God (11:3). The love of our heavenly Father is not based on what we can do for him. It is not conditioned on our perfect obedience. It is a love that allows us to make our own mistakes so that we may grow from them. It is a love that will discipline us so we will become the people we were created to be. The Father's love is something we cannot seek, earn, buy, or deserve. It is a love that desires the very best for us and knows what that best is. "Every good and perfect gift is from above, coming down from the Father of the heavenly lights, who does not change like shifting shadows" (James 1:17).

Fatherlike, he tends and spares us,
Well our feeble frame he knows;
In his hands he gently bears us,
Rescues us from all our foes;
Praise him, praise him,
Praise him, praise him,
Widely as his mercy goes.

—HENRY F. LYTE, 1834 (BASED ON PSALM 103)

Our Father in heaven, hallowed be your name!

$\frac{2}{3}$|27   CREATOR

SCRIPTURE: PSALM 8; ISAIAH 40:25–26, 28

"To whom will you compare me?
> Or who is my equal?" says the Holy One.
Lift your eyes and look to the heavens:
> Who created all these?
He who brings out the starry host one by one,
> and calls them each by name.
Because of his great power and mighty strength,
> not one of them is missing. . . .

Do you not know?
> Have you not heard?
The LORD is the everlasting God,
> the *Creator* of the ends of the earth.

ISAIAH 40:25–26, 28

*W*e like to think we are creative, and indeed we are prolific makers of things. Were we to consider the last hundred years alone, a listing of the human inventions that facilitate transportation, communication, and generally make life easier would fill a book.

To create is "to cause to exist, to bring into being." God alone can truly cause something to exist. God alone can take meaningless nothing, without form and void, and make of it something significant.

It is because we have indeed been created in God's image that we have the capacity to take what we have been given and form from it something fresh.

The conception and subsequent birth of a child is a glorious, creative act that God allows us to participate in. But who really caused that child to exist? Who really brought that child into being?

Using the gifts God has put at our disposal, we as God's image-bearers paint, we compose or perform music, we sculpt, we write, we weave, we knit, we cook, we sew, and sometimes we come up with something that has a fresh sound or a fresh look to it. Our work went into "creation," and people sometimes laud our efforts as creative or imaginative. But the best creations of the image bearers are at most reminders of, and reflections of, our Creator.

> The spacious firmament on high,
> With all the blue ethereal sky,
> And spangled heav'ns, a shining frame,
> Their great Original proclaim.
> Th' unwearied sun, from day to day,
> Does his Creator's pow'r display,

And publishes to ev'ry land
The work of an almighty hand.

Soon as the evening shades prevail,
The moon takes up the wondrous tale,
And nightly to the list'ning earth
Repeats the story of her birth;
Whilst all the stars that round her burn,
And all the planets in their turn,
Confirm the tidings as they roll,
And spread the truth from pole to pole.

What though, in solemn silence, all
Move round this dark terrestrial ball?
What though nor real voice nor sound
Amidst their radiant orbs be found?
In reason's ear they all rejoice,
And utter forth a glorious voice;
For ever singing as they shine,
"The hand that made us is divine."

—JOSEPH ADDISON, 1712 (BASED ON PSALM 19)

Creator God, forgive us for clinging so foolishly to that which we consider "our" creation. Help us to lay these creations and the recognition or lack of recognition they bring us at the feet of the only One truly worthy of the name Creator.

30 OWNER OF THE CATTLE ON A THOUSAND HILLS

SCRIPTURE: PSALM 50:7–12

"I am God, your God. . . .
for every animal of the forest is mine,
    and *the cattle on a thousand hills.*
I know every bird in the mountains,
    and the creatures of the field are mine . . .
    for the world is mine, and all that is in it."

PSALM 50:7, 10–12

And my God will meet all your needs according to his glorious
riches in Christ Jesus.

PHILIPPIANS 4:19

So do not worry, saying, "What shall we eat?" or "What shall
we drink?" or "What shall we wear?" For the pagans run after
all these things, and your heavenly Father knows that you
need them. But seek first his kingdom and his righteousness,
and all these things will be given you as well.

MATTHEW 6:31–33

o four-year-old Justin, the birthday gift from his grandparents was only a small blue piece of paper with some words and numbers on it. With only his four years of experience, he failed to understand that on that small blue piece of paper was a promise that, at his request, a certain bank would make two hundred dollars available to him. Justin failed to understand the generous gift that had been given to him.

How many of us are like Justin! We fail both to appreciate and to appropriate all that our God has put at our disposal! All the power of heaven and earth, peace that defies human understanding, the wherewithal to meet all our needs—these are in the bank for us, and we have a blank check to draw on this account.

What does it mean to be a recipient of God's providence? What are the "incomparable riches of [God's] grace, expressed in his kindness to us in Christ Jesus" (Eph. 2:7)? Like Justin, because we don't always see something tangible in front of us, we underestimate what we have been given. Maybe we need to take the advice of the old hymn and "count [our] many blessings, name them, one by one, And it will surprise [us] what the Lord has done."

A story is told of a retired gentleman who booked passage on a cruise ship bound for Hawaii. Each day of that seven-day cruise he spent in his small cabin, lying on his bunk. He ate nothing but the crackers, peanut butter, and dried prunes he had brought with him. He failed to understand that the sumptuous meals, snacks, lectures and other entertainment, swimming pool, game room, exercise room, library, and deck area were all available to him, included in the fare that had already been paid.

Our fare has already been paid. All of our Lord's considerable resources are available to us for the asking.

> Praise to the Lord, who o'er all things so wondrously reigneth,
> Shelters thee under his wings, yea, so gently sustaineth!
> Hast thou not seen how thy desires e'er have been
> Granted in what he ordaineth?

—JOACHIM NEANDER, 1680

God, our Provider, you dress the field lilies gloriously! You know the number of hairs on our heads. You know what we need. With gratitude we draw on your provisions today.

31   LION OF THE

TRIBE OF JUDAH

SCRIPTURE: JOB 10:16; JEREMIAH 49:19; EZEKIEL 19:1–4;
HOSEA 5:14–15; 11:9–10; 13:4–8; AMOS 3:4;
REVELATION 5:5

Like a lion coming up from Jordan's thickets
    to a rich pastureland,
I [the Lord] will chase Edom from its land in an instant . . .
Who is like me and who can challenge me?
    And what shepherd can stand against me?

JEREMIAH 49:19

Then one of the elders said to me, "Do not weep! See, the *Lion of the tribe of Judah* . . . has triumphed. He is able to open the scroll and its seven seals."

REVELATION 5:5

*T*he King of Beasts! Majestic, powerful, beautiful, awful. We shudder at his roar. We shiver to think of the potential of those claws and teeth. He must never be considered tame.

The One named Lion of the tribe of Judah is the same One the prophet Ezekiel wrote about:

> What a lioness was your mother
>> among the lions!
> She lay down among the young lions
>> and reared her cubs. (19:2)

She nursed them, chased off intruders, and taught them all the ways of a lion.

> She brought up one of her cubs,
>> and he became a strong lion.
> He learned to tear the prey
>> and he devoured men. (19:3)

We are the Lion's adopted cubs—we have been fed, protected, and taught.

Unchallengeable, the Lion chased away his enemies in an instant. No mere shepherd dares stand against him (Jer. 49:19). And we are the Lion's cubs!

The Lion's cubs forget who feeds them and become proud. Since cubs are the privileged progeny of the Lion, they are the ones he loves enough to punish. The Lion destroys his enemies but punishes his cubs so that "in their misery they will earnestly seek [him]" (Hos. 5:15).

Sometimes a cub holds his head high, thinking for a moment that he is the King instead of the cub. At such a time, the Lion stalks his own cub and again displays his awesome power (Job 10:16).

C. S. Lewis, in his Chronicles of Narnia, paints a wonderful picture of Aslan, the Great Lion:

> "Ooh!" said Susan, "I'd thought he was a man. Is he—quite safe? I shall feel rather nervous about meeting a lion."
>
> "That you will, dearie, and no mistake," said Mrs. Beaver. "If there's anyone who can appear before Aslan without their knees knocking, they're either braver than most, or just silly."
>
> "Then he isn't safe?" said Lucy.
>
> "Safe?" said Mr. Beaver. "Don't you hear what Mrs. Beaver tells you? Who said anything about safe? 'Course he isn't safe. But he's good. He's the King, I tell you."[4]

Good and terrible Lion, "You are worthy ... to receive glory and honor and power, for you created all things, and by your will they were created and have their being." (Rev. 4:11)

32 A CONSUMING FIRE

SCRIPTURE: MALACHI 3:1–4

Our God is a *consuming fire*.

HEBREWS 12:29

Then suddenly the Lord you are seeking will come to his temple . . . But who can endure the day of his coming? Who can stand when he appears? For he will be like a refiner's fire . . . He will sit as a refiner and purifier of silver; he will purify the Levites and refine them like gold and silver. Then the Lord will have men who will bring offerings in righteousness.

MALACHAI 3:1–3

By day the LORD went ahead of them in a pillar of cloud to guide them on their way and by night in a pillar of fire to give them light, so they could travel by day or night. Neither the pillar of cloud by day nor the pillar of fire by night left its place in front of the people.

EXODUS 13:21–22

The neon lights of our city streets pale in comparison to the brilliance of God. No human invention could have lit up the sky like God's towering inferno!

The pillar of fire, although it was probably regarded with reverence, did not strike terror in the hearts of the Israelites who saw it. A mother, putting her little one to bed, could provide assurance to her child. The fiery night light at the entrance of the camp meant that God himself was with them, watching as they slept. If ever the desert night grew chill, God's fire was their warmth. Sometimes night travel was a welcome relief from travel during the desert's daytime heat. The fiery pillar would lead the way, showing the Israelites where they were to go. They did not need to carry torches. The pillar of fire provided light and direction. Every night God's fire would be there with them. His people could count on it. The pillar of fire was their comfort.

The God who is a comforting fire is also a consuming fire. The fire of God fell from heaven and utterly devoured the water-drenched sacrifice of God's prophet, Elijah (1 Kings 18:38).

Our God is also like a refiner's fire. Only a very small percentage of each chunk of ore is pure gold. The ore is full of impurities. To extract the gold so that it can be used, the ore must be placed in a furnace and subjected to tremendous temperatures. At last, the once solid ore melts, and the gold can be separated.

There is a comforting aspect to this Consuming Fire. It is not the sons of Jacob the Cheat who are consumed (Mal. 3:6)—it is their impurity and sin. Being melted and having all but the gold stripped away, then being melted again and shaped—it is a painful process. But the Refiner knows what he is about.

When through fiery trials thy pathway shall lie,

My grace, all sufficient, shall be thy supply.

The flame shall not hurt thee; I only design

Thy dross to consume, and thy gold to refine.

—"K" in Rippon's *Selection*, 1787

What can be our response? The writer of Hebrews suggests, "Let us be thankful, and so worship God acceptably with reverence and awe, for our 'God is a consuming fire'" (Heb. 12:28–29).

God of Consuming Fire, you who burn away our impurities, you who light our way, you who warm our hearts, receive our gratitude this day.

33 MAN OF SORROWS

SCRIPTURE: ISAIAH 53

> He was despised and rejected by men,
>> a *man of sorrows*, and familiar with suffering.
> Like one from whom men hide their faces
>> he was despised, and we esteemed him not.

ISAIAH 53:3

The process of being booked is completely deperson-alizing. One's wallet, watch, and other possessions are confiscated. Often one's own clothing must be exchanged for institutional garb. Finger printing is required. Even one's own name must be exchanged for an identifying number. This impersonal number must be held high while the police photographer takes mug shots. The details are placed in the official police record. The one who is booked is now numbered with the transgressors.

The Man of Sorrows was "numbered with the transgressors" (Isa. 53:12). In the divine record, he was booked for all the sins of all humankind. He understands well the stigma and the humiliation attached.

He was despised and rejected by men,
    a man of sorrows, and familiar with suffering.
Like one from whom men hide their faces . . . (Isa. 53:3)

Worse still, the Man of Sorrows knows the indescribable horror of having God hide his face. "My God, my God, why have you forsaken me?" he cried (Matt. 27:46).

Playwright Thornton Wilder spoke more truth than perhaps he realized when in *Our Town* he wrote, "In love's service, only the wounded can serve." The Man of Sorrows came to be pierced, crushed, and wounded (Isa. 53:5). And he came because he loved us.

The suffering, the sorrow, and the wounds we sometimes experience pale in contrast to those of the Man of Sorrows. It hardly seems appropriate to use the same words to describe them. But the Man of Sorrows doesn't turn from us. He knows what we feel. He, of all who ever walked this earth, knows how to empathize with us. He became sin for us, and in so doing, our tears became his tears; our grief, his grief; and our pain, his pain. And "by his wounds we are healed" (Isa. 53:5). He took the permanence out of pain.

Man of Sorrows! What a name
For the Son of God, who came
Ruined sinners to reclaim;
Hallelujah! What a Savior!

Bearing shame and scoffing rude,
In my place condemned he stood,
Sealed my pardon with his blood.
Hallelujah! What a Savior!

Guilty, vile, and helpless, we;
Spotless Lamb of God was he;
Full atonement! Can it be?
Hallelujah! What a Savior!

Lifted up was he to die,
"It is finished!" was his cry:
Now in heaven exalted high:
Hallelujah! What a Savior!

When he comes, our glorious King,
All his ransomed home to bring;
Then anew this song we'll sing:
Hallelujah! What a Savior!

—Philip P. Bliss (1838–1876)

Man of Sorrows, we kneel before you this day and exclaim, "What a Savior!"

$\frac{5}{34}$ EL SHADDAI

SCRIPTURE: GENESIS 43:14; PSALM 131:2–3

When Abram was ninety-nine years old, the LORD appeared to
him and said, "I am God Almighty [*El Shaddai*] . . . I have made
you a father of many nations. I will make you very fruitful; I will
make nations of you, and kings will come from you."

GENESIS 17:1, 5–6

And may God Almighty [*El Shaddai*] grant you mercy before
the man so that he will let your other brother and Benjamin
come back with you.

GENESIS 43:14

Because of your father's God [the *el*], who helps you,
 because of the Almighty [*Shaddai*], who blesses you
with blessings of the heavens above,
 blessings of the deep that lies below,
 blessings of the breast and womb.

GENESIS 49:25

But Zion said, "The LORD has forsaken me,
 the LORD has forgotten me."

"Can a mother forget the baby at her breast
 and have no compassion on the child she has borne?

Though she may forget,
>   I will never forget you!
See, I have engraved you on the palms of my hands."

ISAIAH 49:14–16

But I have stilled and quieted my soul;
>   like a weaned child with its mother,
>   like a weaned child is my soul within me.

O Israel, put your hope in the LORD.

PSALM 131:2–3

O Jerusalem, Jerusalem, you who kill the prophets and stone those sent to you, how often I have longed to gather your children together, as a hen gathers her chicks under her wings, but you were not willing.

MATTHEW 23:37

In somewhat the same way as God is bigger than any and all of the names we can name him, he is also bigger than the images our minds conjure of a single gender. Scripture, in showing us facets of who God is, sometimes portrays him in terms we associate with the feminine gender.

The Hebrew name *El Shaddai* comes as close to capturing this aspect of God as does any of his names. The traditional translations of Scripture have consistently rendered this name "Almighty." But to appreciate its full flavor, it will be helpful to examine its Hebrew roots.[5] *El* is a shortened form of *Elohim*. It sets forth the might, the strength, and the excellence of God. *Shad* is the Hebrew word for "breast." *Shaddai* pictures God's fullness or bounty, his tenderness, his generosity, his desire to nurture us and make us fruitful. In one name, God's attributes of might and tenderness are brought together!

When Abram was ninety-nine years old, El Shaddai appeared to him and said, "I have made you a father" (Gen. 17:5). Speaking in strictly human terms, it takes a woman to go to a man and say, "I'm going to make you a father!" Sometimes this announcement comes as a shock. Often the shocking aspect of this news is mingled with a great deal of joy and thanksgiving, along with some apprehension. Certainly all of these emotions were present as El Shaddai's announcement was received. "You will be very fruitful and kings will come from you" (Gen. 17:6, paraphrase).

It was Elohim Shaddai who gave birth to the nation of Israel. The prophet Isaiah described the birthing process thus: "Like a woman in childbirth I cry out, I gasp and pant" (42:14).

Jacob is full of anxiety as he is about to send his beloved son Benjamin off to Egypt in response to the whimsical demand of the ruler who dispensed food. "May [El Shaddai] grant you mercy before the man," he cries (Gen. 43:14).

Later, as Jacob is pronouncing God's blessing on his son Joseph, he says, "Because of the El and the Shaddai, may you have blessings of the breast and the womb" (Gen. 49:25, paraphrase).

Isaiah, in describing the love of God, says it is greater than that of a nursing mother. A unique bonding occurs as the mother holds her child close to her breast. She is the source of all the infant needs for nourishment as she holds the child close to the warmth of her body, within the sound of her heartbeat and secure in the safety of her arms.

A further dimension to this picture is added by the psalmist in Psalm 131. The psalmist feels like a weaned child. "*Why* am I being deprived of what, from my point of view, seems so good and so right?" he may have been asking himself. "This is what I need, God. Why can't I have it?"

Have you ever asked God these sorts of questions?

God, who, like a mother, knows that the growing child must move beyond breast milk, still holds the child close enough to hear the divine heartbeat, allowing the child the warmth and security of being held tightly in divine arms.

Children's questions may still be unanswered. But their souls are stilled and quieted "like a weaned child with its mother" (Ps. 131:2), because they know, without any doubt, who is holding them!

El Shaddai, almighty, tender God, hold us close to your heart today.

35 ADVOCATE

SCRIPTURE: HEBREWS 2:16; 4:15–16

> My little children, I am writing this to you so that you may
> not sin; but if any one does sin, we have an *advocate* with the
> Father, Jesus Christ the righteous.
>
> 1 JOHN 2:1 RSV

What if you had to stand before the great eternal Judge and present your own case? Imagine yourself, standing alone at the bar, clothed in your own very best efforts. The prosecutor is a shrewd one. He has all the resources of hell itself to draw on. The key exhibit in this case is your own obedience to the law of God. What would the verdict be?

Scripture leaves no room for question. "All have sinned and fall short of the glory of God," writes the apostle Paul (Rom. 3:23). Guilty.

But we don't have to present our own case. We have an Advocate, one who stands in our place to speak on our behalf. Our Advocate has the necessary qualifications. He is familiar with our case and has been since before the earth was founded (Isa. 40:21–28).

Our Advocate prepares his clients. He knows that, dressed in our own righteousness, we don't stand a chance. At great personal cost, he has seen to it that appropriate clothing has been provided to us.

A certain defendant awaited the day of his trial in jail. He was scheduled to appear before a judge who was known for his fastidious attention to proper courtroom dress and decorum. Male defendants who appeared before him were expected to wear a coat and tie. But this defendant did not own a coat or tie and had no means of procuring them. Before the appointed hour of the trial, the defendant received the appropriate clothing, specially delivered to him. The clothing had been sent by the judge himself, from his personal wardrobe.

When we stand before God, we will be able to stand there in clothing provided from the Judge's own wardrobe. We will be able to wear the righteousness of God himself!

When we stand before God, we will not need to stand alone. Our Advocate, Jesus Christ the Righteous, will be standing with us. He will plead our case, and already we can rejoice in the verdict.

> My advocate appears for my defense on high;
> The Father bows his ears and lays his thunder by.
> Not all that hell or sin can say
> Shall turn his heart, his love away.
>
> —ISAAC WATTS, 1709

Jesus, our Advocate, our case is totally without merit, except that we may claim your righteousness. Stand with us today!

⟫ | 36 FAITHFUL WITNESS

SCRIPTURE: REVELATION 1:1–6; JOHN 1:1–3; 11:25 14:6, 9;
1 CORINTHIANS 15:55–57; EPHESIANS 2:12–13;
ACTS 1:8

> Grace and peace to you . . . from Jesus Christ, who is the
> *faithful witness*, the firstborn from the dead, and the ruler of
> the kings of the earth.
>
> REVELATION 1:5

*W*hat is a good witness?

A good witness is someone who was there. Someone who can accurately and faithfully attest to what he or she experienced, saw, tasted, and felt. A good witness often has a credible record, someone who has proven reliable in the past. A good witness will often impact the verdict.

Translators of Scripture ordinarily consider the oldest manuscripts to be the most reliable. They look for the testimony closest in time to the event or statement. But there is nothing secondhand or circumstantial about the testimony of Jesus Christ, Faithful Witness. The apostle John indicates at the beginning of his Gospel that this witness was present with God from the beginning. He testifies to the whole truth of God, and nothing but the truth. We can count on this testimony to be faithful and accurate. When this witness assures us that whoever believes in him will live, even though he dies, that testimony has the ring of authenticity. For this witness has felt the sting of death. The dead body of this witness was buried. Then this witness, himself, was the first to be raised from the dead.

Jesus Christ, Faithful Witness, has signed his word in blood. This has impacted the verdict! We are freed from our sins. And there is even more: we are no longer illegal aliens but kingdom citizens.

We are priests, John continues as he relates the testimony of this witness. What does that mean for us? It means we have access at any time to the presence of the God we serve. We require no special introduction, and we need not schedule an appointment through some secretary.

In the person of this witness we see the face of the God who loves us. Because of his reliability in the past, we can trust him concerning our future. His Spirit even empowers us to be witnesses on his behalf!

You, Jesus Christ, are the Faithful Witness! You are the reliable word. To you be glory and power for ever and ever!

$\frac{s}{2}$| 37 BRIDEGROOM

SCRIPTURE: ISAIAH 62:5

> As a *bridegroom* rejoices over his bride,
>   so will your God rejoice over you.
>
> ISAIAH 62:5

> The bride belongs to the *bridegroom*. The friend who attends
> the *bridegroom* waits and listens for him, and is full of joy
> when he hears the *bridegroom's* voice. That joy is mine, and it
> is now complete.
>
> JOHN 3:29

*I*n our twenty-first-century society, traditional weddings tend to focus on the bride. The bride's family issues the invitations, plans and pays for the reception, and hosts the wedding. When the wedding processional begins, all eyes look in the direction of the approaching bride. Few even notice, until after the fact, that the groom has also entered to the accompaniment of the same music!

But a marriage ceremony was very different in Middle Eastern cultures during the time when the Scriptures were being written.

The bridegroom and his family hosted the wedding. This is clear from the account of the wedding at Cana, where Jesus did his first miracle (John 2:1–11)—the bridegroom supplied the wine. It is also indicated in a parable Jesus told (Matt. 22:2). A king prepared a wedding banquet for his son. The wedding invitations were personally delivered by servants from the bridegroom's household.

The bridegroom is the key figure in the wedding procession (Matt. 25:1–10). All the attendants are to be in readiness for the bridegroom's arrival. The psalmist compares the sun to "a bridegroom coming forth from his pavilion" (Ps. 19:5). The bridegroom arrival is a glorious moment, and from that point on, the excitement crescendos.

The bridegroom has gone to great personal expense and effort in order that this wedding could take place. In preparation, "a bridegroom adorns his head like a priest" (Isa. 61:10). A priest's head was anointed with oil as a symbol that he was set apart for the special purpose of offering sacrifices to God on behalf of the people. Our Bridegroom, Jesus Christ, is worthy of the adornment of a priest. He has offered the supreme sacrifice—himself—on behalf of his bride.

Our Bridegroom has even provided clothing for the bride to wear: "fine linen, bright and clean" (Rev. 19:8).

The bride eyes not her garment, but her dear bridegroom's face;
[She] will not gaze at glory, but on [her] King of grace;
Not at the crown He gifteth, but on His pierced hand:
The Lamb is all the glory of Emmanuel's land.

—Anne R. Cousin, 1857, based upon
Samuel Rutherford (1600–1661)

The wedding supper will certainly be the wedding feast to end all wedding feasts. The angel who described the plans for the celebration to the apostle John said that those who were invited were blessed (Rev. 19:9).

There will be a great multitude at this wedding, all at the invitation of the Father of the Bridegroom, God himself! They will greet the arrival of the Bridegroom with shouting that sounds like the roar of rushing waters and peals of loud thunder.

Hallelujah!
For our Lord God Almighty reigns.
Let us rejoice and be glad
and give him glory!
For the wedding of the Lamb has come,
and his bride has made herself ready. (Rev. 19:6–7)

O Jesus Christ, our Bridegroom! Help us to prepare for your coming with the meticulous care of a bride-to-be. Help us to anticipate your coming with the enthusiasm of a bride-to-be. Come, Lord Jesus.

38   PRINCE OF PEACE

SCRIPTURE: EPHESIANS 2:11–18

And he will be called . . .
> *Prince of Peace.*

ISAIAH 9:6

And the peace of God, which transcends all understanding,
will guard your hearts and your minds in Christ Jesus.

PHILIPPIANS 4:7

Peace I leave with you; my peace I give you. I do not give to
you as the world gives. Do not let your hearts be troubled and
do not be afraid.

JOHN 14:27

I have told you these things, so that in me you may have peace.
In this world you will have trouble. But take heart! I have
overcome the world.

JOHN 16:33

But the fruit of the Spirit is . . . peace.

GALATIANS 5:22

*S*ee if you can paint in your mind a picture of peace. Most of us will visualize a quiet, tranquil, well-ordered scene with an absence of any sort of conflict. But when we look at the picture of the Prince of Peace presented in Scripture, it shatters our mental images.

It is noteworthy that the very first promise of the One who would come and who would be called Prince of Peace states that "he will crush [Satan's] head" (Gen. 3:15). The apostle Paul picks up on this image in Romans 16:20: "The God of peace will soon crush Satan under your feet. The grace of our Lord Jesus be with you." Crushing someone underfoot is hardly a tranquil activity. The act of crushing seems more warlike than peaceful. Paul describes the believer by using the metaphor of a soldier putting on his armor in preparation for battle. The soldier's footwear is to be the "readiness that comes from the gospel of peace" (Eph. 6:15).

Perhaps one reason for the apparent contradiction is that we have lost some of the original Hebrew meaning for the word. The root of the Hebrew *shalom* or *shalam* (peace) may originally have signified oneness, completeness, or perfection.[6]

If peace involves perfection, is there hope for any of us? Listen to the words of Jesus: "Peace I leave with you; my peace I give you" (John 14:27). Christ Jesus offers us the perfection of his heart! God sees Christ's perfection and considers us perfect in him. Like a strong magnet pulls scattered bits of iron into line with itself, so his strong and perfect heart pulls our hearts into conformity with his.

In order to restore our oneness with God, in order to perfect us and make us complete, the greatest act of violence in all of history was committed. A superficial glossing over of the problem of sin would not have sufficed. God had to cut through to its very heart in order to purchase our peace.

> He was pierced for our transgressions,
>> he was crushed for our iniquities;
> the punishment that brought us peace was upon him,
>> and by his wounds we are healed. (Isa. 53:5)

The price of our peace was enormous.

The Prince of Peace did not come to smooth ruffled feathers. Not at the personal, national, or international level. His is a peace that starts in the heart and works its way outward, never the other way around. That is why it is a peace that "transcends all understanding" (Phil 4:7). The people around us look at the superficial circumstances that surround us. They can't understand what is going on in the heart of a child of God. Human understanding would have us believe that peace must work from the outside in.

The word *shalom* is even today used as a greeting by the Jewish people. The apostle Paul used it as a greeting and closing in most of his letters. And Jesus said, "Peace be with you" as he appeared to his assembled disciples after his death and resurrection (Luke 24:36). But when Jesus, Prince of Peace, uses the greeting *shalom*, it is far more than an intangible greeting or a wish. It is a gift. It is the gift of the Person who himself is Peace.

I am who you need. I am your perfection. I am your completeness. I am your reconciliation. I am your peace—this is the message of Jesus Christ, Prince of Peace.

The God of Peace is still engaged in less than tranquil activity, and we are still confronted with less than tranquil circumstances. But the price of our peace has already been paid. The promised Peace who has begun to work in the hearts of the children of God will one day work his way outward. The result will be that men will beat their swords into plowshares, and the lion will lie down with the lamb.

May the God of peace, who through the blood of the eternal covenant brought back from the dead our Lord Jesus, that great Shepherd of the sheep, equip [us] with everything good for doing his will, and may he work in us what is pleasing to him, through Jesus Christ, to whom be glory for ever and ever. (Heb. 13:20–21)

"Peace be with you."
"And with you."*

---

* If you are using this with a group, it might be meaningful to "pass the peace" around your group. Each person says to the next, "Peace be with you." The person addressed responds, "And with you," until this greeting has gone all around the group.

39 LIVING BREAD

SCRIPTURE: JOHN 6:1–14, 25–59; 1 CORINTHIANS 11:23–24

Then Jesus declared, "I am the bread of life. He who comes to me will never go hungry."

JOHN 6:35

I am the *living bread* that came down from heaven. If anyone eats of this bread, he will live forever. This bread is my flesh, which I will give for the life of the world.

JOHN 6:51

The Lord Jesus, on the night he was betrayed, took bread, and when he had given thanks, he broke it and said, "This is my body, which is for you; do this in remembrance of me."

1 CORINTHIANS 11:23–24

Bread has been referred to as the staff of life. It is symbolic of the food we need for sustenance—not an optional food, such as pickles, artichokes, or chocolate. Bread is what supports us, nourishes us, and keeps us alive. The fragrance of freshly baked bread is an unspoken invitation few can resist.

In the late eighteenth century, the young queen of France, Marie Antoinette, became notorious for her extravagant lifestyle at a time when her government was facing financial crises.

She is said to have one day asked an official why the Parisians were angry.

"They are hungry and have no bread," was the reply.

She has been remembered throughout two centuries for the insensitive response attributed to her: "Let them eat cake." Nourishment, not just something to fill them up, was what the French people needed.

What a contrast this attitude is to the one shown by Jesus (John 6). A great crowd had followed Jesus around the Sea of Galilee to see the miracles he was performing and to hear his teaching. There were no roadside fast-food restaurants for these people who had walked quite a distance from their homes.

"How shall we feed these people?" Jesus asked his disciples.

"You've got to be kidding," they responded. "We could spend eight months' salary and not have enough to give everyone in this crowd even a bite of bread."

One boy had thought ahead, or perhaps his mother had. He had brought a small lunch with him. Not much. But in the hands of the One who is the Living Bread, that small lunch provided an ample meal for well over five thousand people, with twelve baskets of leftovers.

"I am the bread of life," Jesus said later to some of the people who thought they had located a permanent free lunch ticket. Many didn't understand. They would be hungry again for the kind of food that spoils. But Jesus himself could supply them the kind of nourishment that would permanently quiet the spiritual

NAMES OF GOD

hunger pangs each one had within. Just as people need bread for nourishment, so we need the sustenance Jesus supplies in order to live eternally.

A loaf of bread, golden brown and still warm from the oven, looks beautiful. But in order to do any good for anyone, it must be broken—first with hands or a knife, then with teeth. Finally, the body's digestive juices continue the "breaking down" process in order that the bread may do what it was meant to do.

Jesus, the Living Bread, also had to be broken in order to do what he was meant to do—be life for us. What Jesus offers is not cake—sweet, temporarily filling, but not particularly nourishing. Jesus offers bread—something both desirable and good for us. He offers to be for us what we need to live. He himself is the staff of life—eternal life.

Bread of Heaven, be for us our day's nourishment. You are who we need!

40 THE WORD

SCRIPTURE: JOHN 1:1–18; REVELATION 19:11–16

In the beginning was *the Word*, and *the Word* was with God, and *the Word* was God. He was with God in the beginning.

JOHN 1:1–2

The Word became flesh and made his dwelling among us. We have seen his glory, the glory of the One and Only, who came from the Father, full of grace and truth.

JOHN 1:14

He is dressed in a robe dipped in blood, and his name is *the Word* of God.

REVELATION 19:13

Friends of a young man had told him about a girl they thought he should meet. They showed him a picture of her. He was interested, but many miles separated them. How could he get to know her at such a distance? He sent her a letter, telling her in his own words who he was, what he valued, and what his goals were. And she wrote back. The young man's most effective means of communicating what he was like was his word.

God has given us the testimony of friends. God has given us pictures—think of some of the names we have considered: Bread, Door, Star, Lamb, Vine. But his most effective expression of who he himself is, is his Word, Jesus Christ.

The right word enhances our understanding. It strips away the fog that surrounds a difficult or abstract concept. It can cut through a broad generality, making it clear that the speaker means A, not B or C.

The right word, from the right person, can be all that is necessary to establish credibility. "Give me your word, and I'll believe it."

The word is a reflection of what is in the heart. "Out of the overflow of [the] heart [the] mouth speaks," says Luke (6:45). The living Word was with God and was God from the beginning. He is the overflow of the abundant love that is the essence of the heart of God.

The living Word is God's best expression of himself. The Word clarifies who God is for us and enhances our understanding. The living Word is the best evidence for God's credibility.

Think of the power an ordinary word has in certain contexts: a jury foreman announces guilty; a young woman replies yes; the umpire calls strike; a congress declares war. The power of the living Word far exceeds the power of even these words. We need not fear a world filled with devils or the rage of the prince of darkness, for "one little Word shall fell him."

That Word above all earthly powers,
    No thanks to them, abideth;
The Spirit and the gifts are ours
    Through him who with us sideth;
Let goods and kindred go,
    This mortal life also;
The body they may kill:
    God's truth abideth still;
His kingdom is forever.

—MARTIN LUTHER, 1529

A word, once spoken, cannot be unsaid. God has expressed himself in the incarnate Word. He cannot and will not reverse himself. That Word is with us forever.

Come, thou Incarnate Word, Gird on thy mighty sword, Our prayer attend: Come and thy people bless, And give thy Word success ... Amen.

—Anonymous, c. 1757

41 | ROSE OF SHARON

Scripture: Song of Solomon 2:1

I am a *rose of Sharon*,
a lily of the valleys.

Song of Songs 2:1

The rose of Sharon is a large hibiscus shrub. It grows about twelve feet tall, has large three-lobed leaves, and a lovely rose, purple, white, or blue flower.

The uniqueness of the rose of Sharon lies in the fact that it blooms at an unlikely time and in unlikely places. The rose blossoms in the fall, when few other shrubs are in bloom. It grows well in unfavorable conditions and does not seem to be partial to the city or the country.

Unfavorable growing conditions? In our honest moments we sometimes marvel that the soil of our lives could produce anything beautiful. It is full of the stones of selfishness, the weeds of deceitfulness, and the acidity of our pride. Yet the Rose of Sharon persists, blooms, and grows, even when other plants are dormant.

Lo, how a rose upspringing
On tender root has grown:
A rose by prophet's singing
To all the world made known.
The Rose 'midst winter's cold
A lovely blossom bearing,
In former days foretold.

This Flow'r whose fragrance tender
With sweetness fills the air,
Dispels with glorious splendor
The darkness everywhere.
True Man, yet very God;
From sin and death he saves us
And lightens every load.

—GERMAN AUTHOR, UNKNOWN (C. 1500)

Jesus, Rose of Sharon, you startle and amaze us by being present at unlikely times and in unlikely places. These are the times and places we most need to see you. Bloom in our hearts today so that the lives of those around us may be touched by the beauty and fragrance of your love. Those who know us will wonder that such poor soil could produce such a flower. They will know is is the tenacity of the flower, not the quality of the soil. Receive our praise!

42 HOLY, HOLY, HOLY

SCRIPTURE: ISAIAH 6:1–8; EXODUS 33:17–23; 1 PETER 1:15–16

> *Holy, holy, holy* is the LORD Almighty;
> the whole earth is full of his glory.
>
> ISAIAH 6:3

> Day and night they never stop saying:
> "*Holy, holy, holy*
> is the Lord God Almighty,
> who was, and is, and is to come."
>
> REVELATION 4:8

In all of Scripture this is the one name or attribute of God that is named three times in succession. The emphasis cannot be accidental. God is so named by the four living creatures in Revelation and by the seraphim in Isaiah's vision. There are other names of God that are much easier for us to think about. If we are honest, this one makes us a little squeamish.

As we look at this name of God, the nearer we approach, and the more clearly we see, the more uncomfortable we become. To look at God's holiness is something like looking with unshaded eyes directly at the sun. God told Moses that no one could see his face and live. God covered Moses with his hand and allowed him to see his back. Moses' face shone as a result of this encounter.

The early Israelites were so conscious of God's holiness that they would never speak his name aloud, or write it, except in abbreviated form. We, on the other hand, sometimes are so casual that we lose the impact of what it means for the Holy, Holy, Holy God to make himself one with sinful human beings. No analogy can do justice to the reality of God's incarnation for the purpose of our atonement, but perhaps we can begin to think in the right direction if we imagine a beautifully and carefully made white wedding dress being drenched in the sewer. Or imagine your thirteen-year-old daughter being raped. But because God is God, the sewer and the rape did not ruin him.

Not only is God holy, but he expects us to be holy also (1 Peter 1:15–16). Sometimes it seems more socially acceptable to be a little less than holy. Being holy doesn't always sound like a lot of fun. Sometimes being holy seems like an impossible achievement. It would be, if we had to do it by ourselves!

We have met the Holy, Holy, Holy God. Such an encounter must have one of two results: blasphemy or worship. Isaiah worshiped. In Isaiah 6 he catches a glimpse of the Holy God in a service of worship that begins with adoration and praise. Isaiah confesses his sin and is then assured of God's pardon. The Word of the Lord is proclaimed and Isaiah responds. The outgrowth of his worship is service. Service that does not spring from having worshiped, as Isaiah's did, soon becomes meaningless.

Holy, Holy, Holy God, like Isaiah, when we are confronted with your holiness, we become more acutely aware of our own sinfulness. We acknowledge it and we confess it. Help us to forsake our sin, to the end that we may obey your command to be holy, even as you are holy.

Holy, Holy, Holy God in three persons. We are full of wonder that you have made atonement for our sin.

Holy, Holy, Holy God. With Isaiah, we respond to your word, "Here am I. Send me!" (Isa. 6:8).

43 FRIEND OF TAX COLLECTORS AND SINNERS

SCRIPTURE: LUKE 7:34–50

> The Son of Man came eating and drinking, and they say,
> "Here is . . . a *friend of tax collectors and 'sinners.'*"
>
> MATTHEW 11:19

> But there is a friend who sticks closer than a brother.
>
> PROVERBS 18:24

> Greater love has no one than this, that he lay down his life for
> his friends.
>
> JOHN 15:13

Even more hated than the Roman conquerors were the tax collectors. The tax collector was no foreigner. He might have had a farm just down the road. He might have been Uncle Ezra's second cousin. A greedy tax collector (and most of them were) could demand not only the revenue required by Rome but also an additional amount to line his own pockets. He could get away with this because he was backed by Roman soldiers, who could, if necessary, be very persuasive! Such a collector turned his back on his friends in exchange for cash and clout.

Yet as Jesus was passing through Jericho one day, it was a tax collector he singled out from the crowd. It was a tax collector with whom Jesus chose to have lunch. As a result of Jesus' gracious friendship, Zacchaeus the tax collector became a changed man (Luke 19:1–10).

Matthew, another tax collector, was chosen to be part of Jesus' inner circle. He was one of the twelve who walked, worked, watched, ate, slept, and lived with Jesus during his time of ministry on earth. This collector of taxes later used his record-keeping ability to become a chronicler of the life of Jesus, his friend.

Jesus also openly aquainted himself with sinners. In a culture which didn't view any woman very highly, Jesus befriended "used" women. One prostitute was overwhelmed by the compassion she had experienced and the forgiveness she knew she had received from God. This broken woman poured on Jesus' feet her tears of repentance, together with the costly perfume from her broken jar (Luke 7:36–50). She had been made whole.

Then there was the foreign woman who slept around. She came to the well for her daily water supply at a time when none of the other women would be there, probably because they would look down their noses at her. Jesus befriended this woman as well. She became a new person (John 4:1–26).

Fellow friends of Jesus! Look around you at the company we are in! Prostitutes, cheaters, liars—Jesus even called Judas his friend (Matt. 26:50). Just as there is nothing we ourselves can do to be worthy of his friendship, so there is nothing we can do to make ourselves ineligible for it.

The friendship has been offered. Jesus has extended his nail-scarred hand to us. All we need to do is take it, and like the tax collectors and sinners before us, we won't ever be the same!

Lord Jesus, today we join hands and hearts with the great company of sinners you have made your friends. Receive our gratitude, we pray.

44 | OMEGA

SCRIPTURE: PSALM 102:25–28; PSALM 46

I am . . . the *Omega*, . . . the Last, . . . the End.

REVELATION 22:13

But you [God] remain the same,
and your years will never end.

PSALM 102:27

So much of that with which we involve ourselves has an end. We spend ourselves preparing for a special visitor or a special occasion. The visit always ends and the occasion is soon over. Time itself has an end. But God? Why does our eternal God name himself with the last letter of the Greek alphabet, omega? What can the name *Omega* tell us about God?

Sometimes advertisers use the phrase "the last word in . . . [whatever they are trying to sell]." They wish to convey the idea that after we have investigated every other similar product, we will find this one to be superior. Nothing else can surpass it.

Sometimes a person is said to have had "the last word" in a discussion or debate. The idea is that after everyone else has had their say and has presented their best argument, this one's word prevailed.

What does it mean to belong to the Omega God? What does it mean to be part of the unending ending? C. S. Lewis gives us a hint as he concludes the last of his Chronicles of Narnia:

> For us this is the end of all the stories, and we can most truly say that they all lived happily ever after. But for them it was only the beginning of the real story. All their life in this world and all their adventures in Narnia had only been the cover and the title page: now at last they were beginning Chapter One of the Great Story, which no one on earth has read: which goes on for ever: in which every chapter is better than the one before.[7]

Our chief end is to glorify God and to enjoy him *forever*, says the Westminster Catechism. Are we so immersed in our lives today that we never stop to think about what our worshiping will be like in 100 years? Or what it will be like in 1,000 years? Or how about 479,502 years from now?

Belonging to the Omega God means that our worship takes on eternal significance. Our task of inviting others to worship—our families, our neighbors, our co-workers—takes on eternal significance. And our task of equipping ourselves and others to be better worshipers is eternally significant.

You who precede all, nothing and no one will ever surpass you! Omega God, when all other words have been spoken, your Word prevails!

Help us, Omega God—you who precede all beginnings and succeed all endings—help us to look beyond the needs and demands of today. Equip us to better worship you, Omega God, the Last, the everlasting One.

JOIN ALL THE GLORIOUS NAMES!

This is a listing, in alphabetical order, of the names of God and the Scripture passages where they are found. The names are from the New International Version, unless otherwise noted.

I am indebted to Virgil and Carol Olson of Pasadena, California, for their assistance in compiling this list.

Abba . . . . Romans 8:15

Advocate . . . . 1 John 2:1 (KJV)

Almighty . . . . Psalm 68:14

Alpha . . . . Revelation 22:13

Amen . . . . Revelation 3:14

Ancient of Days . . . . Daniel 7:9

Anointed One . . . . Psalm 2:2

Apostle and High Priest . . Hebrews 3:1

Arm of the Lord . . . . Isaiah 53:1

Author of Life . . . . Acts 3:15

Author of Our Faith . . . . Hebrews 12:2

Beginning and the End . . Revelation 21:6

Blessed and Only Ruler . . 1 Timothy 6:15

Branch . . . . Jeremiah 33:15

Bread of God . . . . John 6:33

Bread of Life . . . . John 6:35

Bridegroom . . . . Isaiah 62:5

Bright Morning Star . . Revelation 22:16

Chief Shepherd . . . . 1 Peter 5:4

Chosen One . . . . Isaiah 42:1

Christ . . . . Matthew 22:42

Christ Jesus Our Lord . . . Romans 6:23

Christ of God . . . . Luke 9:20

Christ the Lord . . . . Luke 2:11

Christ, the Son of
  the Living God . . . . . Matthew 16:16

Comforter . . . . John 14:26 (kjv)

Commander . . . . Isaiah 55:4

Consolation of Israel . . . . . Luke 2:25

Consuming Fire . . . Deuteronomy 4:24;
  . . . . Hebrews 12:29

Cornerstone . . . . Isaiah 28:16
Counselor . . . . John 14:26
Creator . . . . 1 Peter 4:19
Deliverer . . . . Romans 11:26
Desired of All Nations . . . Haggai 2:7
Door . . . . John 10:7 (kjv)
El Shaddai . . . . Genesis 17:1 (Hebrew)
Eternal God . . . . Deuteronomy 33:27
Everlasting Father . . . . . . Isaiah 9:6
Exact Representation of
   His [God's] Being . . . . Hebrews 1:3
Faithful and True . . . . Revelation 19:11
Faithful Witness . . . . . Revelation 1:5
Father . . . . Matthew 6:9
Firstborn Among
   Many Brothers . . . . . Romans 8:29
Firstborn from the Dead . . . Revelation 1:5
Firstborn over
   All Creation . . . . . Colossians 1:15
Firstfruits . . . . 1 Corinthians 15:20, 23
Foundation . . . . . . 1 Corinthians 3:11
Friend of Tax Collectors
   and "Sinners" . . . . . Matthew 11:19
Gentle Whisper . . . . . . 1 Kings 19:12
Gift of God . . . . John 4:10
Glory of the Lord . . . . . . Isaiah 40:5
God . . . . Genesis 1:1
God Almighty . . . . Genesis 17:1
God over All . . . . Romans 9:5
God Who Sees Me . . . . . Genesis 16:13
Good Shepherd . . . . John 10:11
Great High Priest . . . . . Hebrews 4:14
Great Shepherd . . . . . Hebrews 13:20
Guide . . . . Psalm 48:14
Head of the Body . . . . . Colossians 1:18

Head of the Church . . . . Ephesians 5:23
Heir of All Things . . . . . Hebrews 1:2
High Priest Forever . . . . . Hebrews 6:20
Holy One . . . . Acts 2:27
Holy One of Israel . . . . . . Isaiah 49:7
Holy Spirit . . . . John 14:26
Hope . . . . Titus 2:13
Horn of Salvation . . . . Luke 1:69
I Am . . . . Exodus 3:14; John 8:58
Image of God . . . . . 2 Corinthians 4:4
Image of His Person . . . Hebrews 1:3 (kjv)
Immanuel . . . . Isaiah 7:14
Jehovah . . . . Psalm 83:18 (kjv)
Jesus . . . . Matthew 1:21
Judge . . . . . . Isaiah 33:22; Acts 10:42
King . . . . Zechariah 9:9
King Eternal . . . . 1 Timothy 1:17
King of Kings . . . . 1 Timothy 6:15
King of the Ages . . . . Revelation 15:3
Lamb of God . . . . John 1:29
Last Adam . . . . . . 1 Corinthians 15:45
Lawgiver . . . . Isaiah 33:22
Leader . . . . Isaiah 55:4
Life . . . . John 14:6
Light of the World . . . . . . John 8:12
Like an Eagle . . . . Deuteronomy 32:11
Lily of the Valley . Song of Solomon 2:1
Lion of the Tribe
   of Judah . . . . Revelation 5:5
Living Stone . . . . 1 Peter 2:4
Living Water . . . . John 4:10
Lord . . . . John 13:13
Lord God Almighty . . . Revelation 15:3
Lord Jesus Christ . . 1 Corinthians 15:57
Lord of All . . . . Acts 10:36

Lord of Glory . . . . . 1 Corinthians 2:8
Lord of Lords . . . . 1 Timothy 6:15
Lord Our Righteousness . . Jeremiah 23:6
Love . . . . 1 John 4:8
Man of Sorrows . . . . Isaiah 53:3
Master . . . . Luke 5:5
Mediator . . . . 1 Timothy 2:5
Merciful . . . . Jeremiah 3:12
Messenger of the Covenant . . Malachi 3:1
Messiah . . . . John 4:25
Mighty God . . . . Isaiah 9:6
Mighty One . . . . Isaiah 60:16
Nazarene . . . . Matthew 2:23
Offspring of David . . . Revelation 22:16
Omega . . . . Revelation 22:13
Only Begotten Son . . . . John 1:18 (KJV)
Our Passover Lamb . 1 Corinthians 5:7
Our Peace . . . . Ephesians 2:14
Potter . . . . Isaiah 29:16
Power of God . . . . . 1 Corinthians 1:24
Prince of Peace . . . . Isaiah 9:6
Prophet . . . . Acts 3:22
Purifier . . . . Malachi 3:3
Rabboni (Teacher) . . . . . John 20:16
Radiance of God's Glory . . Hebrews 1:3
Redeemer . . . . Job 19:25
Refiner's Fire . . . . Malachi 3:2
Resurrection and the Life . . John 11:25
Righteous One . . . . 1 John 2:1
Rock . . . . 1 Corinthians 10:4
Root of David . . . . . . Revelation 22:16
Rose of Sharon . . Song of Solomon 2:1

Ruler of God's Creation . . Revelation 3:14
Ruler of the Kings
  of the Earth . . . . . . Revelation 1:5
Ruler over Israel . . . . Micah 5:2
Savior . . . . Luke 2:11
Scepter out of Israel . . . Numbers 24:17
Seed . . . . Genesis 3:15
Servant . . . . Isaiah 42:1
Shepherd and Overseer
  of Your Souls . . . . 1 Peter 2:25
Shield . . . . Genesis 15:1
Son of David . . . . Matthew 1:1
Son of God . . . . Matthew 27:54
Son of Man . . . . Matthew 8:20
Son of the Most High . . . . . Luke 1:32
Source of Eternal Salvation . . Hebrews 5:9
Spirit of God . . . . Genesis 1:2
Star out of Jacob . . . . . Numbers 24:17
Stone . . . . 1 Peter 2:8
Sun of Righteousness . . . . Malachi 4:2
Teacher . . . . John 13:13
True Light . . . . John 1:9
True Witness . . . . . . Revelation 3:14
Truth . . . . John 14:6
Vine . . . . John 15:5
Way . . . . John 14:6
Wisdom of God . . . . 1 Corinthians 1:24
Witness . . . . Isaiah 55:4
Wonderful Counselor . . . . Isaiah 9:6
Word . . . . John 1:1
Word of God . . . . Revelation 19:13

✥ | NOTES

1. Taken from "May the Mind of Christ My Savior" and used by permission of the executors of the estate of the Reverend A. C. Barham Gould.

2. Taken from the hymn "We Come, O Christ, to Thee" by E. Margaret Clarkson. © by Inter-Varsity Christian Fellowship of the USA and used by permission of InterVarsity Press, Downers Grove, IL 60515.

3. C. S. Lewis, *The Silver Chair* (New York: Macmillan, 1953), 16–17.

4. C. S. Lewis, *The Lion, the Witch, and the Wardrobe* (London: Collins, 1950), 77.

5. Robert B. Girdlestone, *Synonyms of the Old Testament*, reprint ed. (Grand Rapids: Eerdmans, 1974), 32–34.

6. Ibid., 95–98.

7. C. S. Lewis, *The Last Battle* (New York: Macmillan, 1956), 184.

PART 2

ATTRIBUTES *of* GOD

1 IMMANUEL

> Behold, the virgin shall conceive and bear a Son, and shall call
> His name Immanuel.
>
> ISAIAH 7:14

I have had psychiatrists tell me their schedules are over-loaded with people who find the Christmas season almost more than they can bear because of their loneliness and isolation.

Christmas is God's reminder that we are not alone. God revealed in the life, death, and resurrection of Jesus a reconciling love that rescues us from separation and loneliness. We are not alone; God has come down from Heaven to tell us He loves us!

At this Christmas season you can be assured that Jesus Christ is here. He is here to give us hope, to forgive our sins, to give us a new song, to impart faith, and to heal our spiritual wounds if only we will let Him.

If you are lonely this Christmas, welcome Christ into your life. Then ask Him to help you reach out to someone else who is lonely, and show that person His love.

BILLY GRAHAM
Hope for Each Day[1]

2 CHRIST THE LORD

There is born to you this day in the city of David a Savior, who
is Christ the Lord.

LUKE 2:11

*W*hen the shepherds found the baby wrapped in
swaddling clothes and lying in a manger, they
found "a Savior who is Christ the Lord." He came as a sin offering for mankind. He came as the Savior, the fulfillment of the
Old Testament prophecies as the Messiah; but He came as Lord
of heaven and earth also. . . .

Jesus Christ is the ruling, reigning, sovereign Lord over all.

CHARLES F. STANLEY
God's Way Day by Day[2]

3 FAITHFUL WITNESS

From Jesus Christ, the faithful witness, the firstborn from the dead, and the ruler over the kings of the earth.

To Him who loved us and washed us from our sins in His own blood, and has made us kings and priests to His God and Father, to Him be glory and dominion forever and ever. Amen.

REVELATION 1:5–6

Throughout history there has never been a more faithful witness than Jesus Christ. He was a model of servanthood and portrayed for everyone through His everlasting love how precious we are to our Father God.

We are priests in a lost world with one purpose: to glorify God and bear witness that Jesus Christ is the only answer to life everlasting. May the Holy Spirit so control our lives that we shall count it our highest privilege to manifest our Lord and Savior to a lost world. He is not only the transcendent Diety who created us, He is the One who died on our behalf and was subsequently raised from the dead—the first One who experienced the true resurrection.

JACK COUNTRYMAN

4 | HOPE

They shall obtain joy and gladness,
And sorrow and sighing shall flee away.

ISAIAH 35:10

he black, velvety sky was clear and studded with spar-kling stars that had looked down on earth since the beginning of time. Shepherds appeared to be sitting idly by their flocks but in fact were keeping a sharp lookout for anything or anyone who might harm the sheep entrusted to their care. In the distance, the lights from the town could be seen and the noisy commotion could be heard as more people were coming into the town than the town could hold.

On the clear night air, sound traveled easily and somewhere from the direction of the village inn someone slammed a door. And a baby cried.

The seed of the woman, who would open heaven's gate and welcome any and all who place their faith in Him . . . had been given!

The hope that was born that night continues to radiate down through the years until it envelops your heart and mine.

ANNE GRAHAM LOTZ
God's Story[3]

5 HOLY

He who is mighty has done great things for me,
And holy is His name.

LUKE 1:49

We must never forget that when we celebrate Christ and His birth, we are celebrating the God of heaven and earth.

Some may not submit to His lordship, but that doesn't change the position the Father has given His Son. Jesus is Lord whether recognized or not, and He wants to be Lord of your life.

This is the divine structure God has ordained. . . . Anytime we fail to give Christ His rightful place in our lives—first place— we can miss out on the blessings of God.

CHARLES F. STANLEY
God's Way Day by Day[4]

6   SHEPHERD

The Lord is my shepherd;
> I have everything I need.

PSALM 23:1 NCV

S heep aren't smart. They tend to wander into running creeks for water, then their wool grows heavy and they drown. They need a shepherd to lead them to "calm water" (Psalm 23:2). They have no natural defense—no claws, no horns, no fangs. They are helpless. Sheep need a shepherd with a "rod and . . . walking stick" (Psalm 23:4) to protect them. They have no sense of direction. They need someone to lead them "on paths that are right" (Psalm 23:3).

So do we. We, too, tend to be swept away by waters we should have avoided. We have no defense against the evil lion who prowls about seeking whom he might devour. We, too, get lost.

We need a shepherd. We need a shepherd to care for us and to guide us. And we have one. One who knows us by name.

MAX LUCADO
A Gentle Thunder[5]

7   ADVOCATE

> My little children, these things I write to you, so that you may
> not sin. And if anyone sins, we have an Advocate with the
> Father, Jesus Christ the righteous.
>
> 1 JOHN 2:1

In God's perfect plan, He has chosen to provide His Son to help us be on guard to our sinful tendencies. When Satan charges us with sin, Christ represents us and defends us to the Father. His covering of our sin is manifested in all that He does for us. We truly have an advocate that stands in the gap every hour of every day with our Heavenly Father. Therefore, knowing that Jesus represents us as our advocate with the Father to plead our cause in Heaven's court, let us live in such a way that God will be glorified. Our spirit will be strengthened to live boldly in a lost world that needs to know the love of God.

JACK COUNTRYMAN

8 PRINCE OF PEACE

For unto us a Child is born,
Unto us a Son is given;
And the government will be upon His shoulder.
And His name will be called
Wonderful, Counselor, Mighty God,
Everlasting Father, Prince of Peace.

ISAIAH 9:6

*M*any of us find it hard to read those words without hearing Handel's *Messiah* in our mind. That magnificent music beautifully captures the glorious promise and rich truth of these ancient words.

Israel hoped for, longed for, waited for a messiah who would prove victorious over their military oppressors. Israel anticipated a messiah who would bring peace on earth.

God's Messiah—Jesus His Son—would prove victorious over a greater enemy: sin. God's Messiah would also bring a much greater peace: reconcili-ation between God and man.

Christ can indeed bring peace to any situation. The most difficult circumstance, the most ruthless enemy, the deepest pain—none of these is beyond Christ's reach. He can calm your heart and mind. No one brings peace like Jesus.

HENRY & RICHARD BLACKABY
Discovering God's Daily Agenda[6]

9 | GIFT OF GOD

> Every good action and every perfect gift is from God. These
> good gifts come down from the Creator of the sun, moon, and
> stars, who does not change like their shifting shadows.
>
> JAMES 1:17 NCV

The conclusion is unavoidable: self-salvation simply does not work. Man has no way to save himself.

But Paul announces that God has a way. Where man fails God excels. Salvation comes from heaven downward, not earth upward. "Every good action and every perfect gift is from God" (James 1:17).

Please note: Salvation is God-given, God-driven, God-empowered, and God-originated. The gift is not from man to God. It is from God to man.

MAX LUCADO
In the Grip of Grace[7]

10 FIRSTBORN OVER ALL CREATION

He is the image of the invisible God, the firstborn over all creation. For by Him all things were created that are in heaven and that are on earth, visible and invisible, whether thrones or dominions or principalities or powers. All things were created through Him and for Him.

COLOSSIANS 1:15–16

So many statements in Scripture make plain the fact that God and Christ are one. He is the manifestation of God. The invisible God has become visible to men in Jesus Christ. He is the Head of the natural creation and the new creation, so that He is intimately allied to us. Jesus Christ is the eternal One who was before all creation. The Word proclaims that "all things were created through Him," and that He is before all things. Since Christ is God, He is supreme in rank over all creation. Yet He is not only the transcendent deity who created us, He is the one who died on our behalf and was subsequently raised from the dead. Therefore He is also the firstborn from the dead, the first one who experienced the true resurrection.

JACK COUNTRYMAN

11 SON OF MAN

For even the Son of Man did not come to be served, but to serve, and to give His life a ransom for many.

MARK 10:45

*H*ere's a side to the Christmas story that isn't often told: those soft little hands, fashioned by the Holy Spirit in Mary's womb, were made so that nails might be driven through them. Those baby feet, pink and unable to walk, would one day walk up a dusty hill to be nailed to a cross. That sweet infant's heat with sparkling eyes and eager mouth was formed so that someday men might force a crown of thorns onto it. That tender body, warm and soft, wrapped in swaddling clothes, would one day be ripped open by a spear.

Jesus was born to die.

Don't think I'm trying to put a damper on your Christmas spirit. Far from it—for Jesus' death, though devised and carried out by men with evil intentions, was in no sense a tragedy. In fact, it represents the greatest victory over evil anyone has ever accomplished.

JOHN MACARTHUR
Truth for Today[8]

12   JESUS

Joseph . . . took to him his wife, and did not know her till she had brought forth her firstborn Son. And he called His name Jesus.

MATTHEW 1:24–25

Joseph tanked his reputation. He swapped his *tsadiq* diploma for a pregnant fiancée and an illegitimate son and made the big decision of discipleship. He placed God's plan ahead of his own.

Rather than make a name for himself, he made a home for Christ. And because he did, a great reward came his way. "He called His name Jesus."

Queue up the millions who have spoken the name of Jesus, and look at the person selected to stand at the front of the line. Joseph. Of all the saints, sinners, prodigals, and preachers who have spoken the name, Joseph, a blue-collar, small-town construction worker said it first. He cradled the wrinkle-faced prince of heaven and with an audience of angels and pigs, whispered, "Jesus . . . You'll be called Jesus."

MAX LUCADO
Cure for the Common Life [9]

13 AUTHOR OF OUR FAITH

Looking unto Jesus, the author and finisher of our faith, who for the joy that was set before Him endured the cross, despising the shame, and has sat down at the right hand of the throne of God.

HEBREWS 12:2

Everything begins and ends with Jesus. Through Him we have life. We need to consistently focus on Christ instead of our own circumstances. Christ has done everything necessary for us to endure in our faith. There will be trials, but we are to "count it all joy" (James 1:2). Step by step He goes before us and leads us on. The best is always before us and someday we will meet Him face to face and reign with Him in glory. He is our example and model, for He focused on the "joy that was set before Him." His attention was not on the agonies of the cross, but on the crown; not on the suffering, but on the reward.

JACK COUNTRYMAN

14 | LIGHT OF THE WORLD

> I am the light of the world. He who follows Me shall not walk in darkness....
>
> JOHN 8:12

*T*his December the birthday of Jesus Christ will be celebrated all over the world. It will be celebrated in various ways, in many languages, by people of all races. For a few hours many in the world will stop talking of satellites, rockets, and war. For a few hours they will talk of peace on earth and good will toward men. People will exchange their gifts and talk about the Prince of Peace.

Imagine the scene in Bethlehem two thousand years ago. It was the night of nights, and yet it had begun as every other night had before it.

But it was to become the greatest, most significant night of history. This was the night that would conquer darkness and bring in the day when there would be no more night. This was the night when those who sat in darkness would see a great light. This was the night God brought into the world the One who is "the light of the world." May His light shine in your life this Christmas season!

BILLY GRAHAM
Hope for Each Day[10]

∮ | 15   DELIVERER

And so all Israel will be saved, as it is written:

"The Deliverer will come out of Zion,
And He will turn away ungodliness from Jacob;
For this is My covenant with them,
When I take away their sins."

ROMANS 11:26–27

Seven hundred and fifty years before the birth of our Savior, Isaiah wrote of the Deliverer and Redeemer that would come out of Zion. He came with one purpose and that was to show us the way and deliver us from our sin. Through His life and sacrifice, we have eternal life that is secure and nothing or no one can ever take that away from those who choose to accept Him. Life is filled with many challenges and choices, and we are invited to live in communion with Christ. As Christ delivered Himself up as a sacrifice for our sins, let us live in such a way that each day may be filled with the power and pleasure of His presence. He has promised to deliver us from every problem we may face if we will only trust Him and lean on His shoulders.

JACK COUNTRYMAN

16 HIGH PRIEST

Now this is the main point of the things we are saying: We have such a High Priest, who is seated at the right hand of the throne of the Majesty in the heavens.

HEBREWS 8:1

The Jewish priests daily entered the sanctuary to burn incense and trim the lamps. Once a week they replaced the showbread. Once a year, on the Day of Atonement, the high priest entered God's presence. Clearly, the old covenant did not provide for full fellowship between God and His people.

The blood of Christ changed that, though. His death on the cross was the perfect and complete sacrifice for humanity's sins. In fact, no sin or offense is so great that Jesus' atonement cannot make you clean and holy.

We will face temptations and difficult circumstances. At times our strength may fail and our faith may waiver, but we have this hope: Christ our High Priest forever intercedes for us with the Father. He is victorious over death and sin, and He will bring us victory as well.

HENRY & RICHARD BLACKABY
Discovering God's Daily Agenda[11]

$\maltese$ | 17   REDEEMER

"The Redeemer will come to Zion,
And to those who turn from transgression in Jacob,"
Says the LORD.

ISAIAH 59:20

T he Jewish prophets proclaimed that a redeemer would come out of Zion to be the Helper the people so desperately needed. Today, we are blessed that our Redeemer Jesus Christ came in the form of a man with one purpose, to redeem us from our sin.

When life seems difficult and the race we are running seems all uphill, stop and think, *our Lord redeemed us at a priceless cost.* If He saw in us enough worth for which to pay His life, is it not worthwhile to rise up and try again, walking with Him and worshiping Him who has redeemed us from our sin?

JACK COUNTRYMAN

18   THE LIVING STONE

You come to him, the living Stone. . . . Now to you who believe, this stone is precious.

1 Peter 2:4, 7 NIV

Have you ever denied the Lord?

Denied Him with your silence?

Denied Him with your behavior?

Denied Him by calling yourself a Christian yet not acting like one?

Denied Him by priorities and plans and people and places in your life that are Christ-less?

If you have denied Jesus—and surely all of us have in some way—then you know something of the price Peter paid in shame and humiliation for his denial. Instead of repressing your shame and guilt, will you confess it to the Lord so that you can experience the same forgiveness and restoration that Peter did? When you do, you can share the testimony with Peter and the saints down through the ages who know from their own experience that He is precious! "Speak, Lord, for your servant is listening" (1 Samuel 3:9 NIV).

Anne Graham Lotz
Just Give Me Jesus [12]

19 KING OF KINGS

The Lamb . . . King of kings.

REVELATION 17:14

*F*rom his very birth Christ was recognized as King. Something about Him inspired allegiance, loyalty, and homage. Wise men brought Him gifts. Shepherds fell down and worshiped Him. Herod, realizing that there is never room for two thrones in one kingdom, sought His life.

As Jesus began His ministry, His claims upon people's lives were total and absolute. He demanded and received complete adoration and devotion. Mature men and women left their businesses and gave themselves in complete obedience to Him. Many of them gave their lives, pouring out the last full measure of devotion.

He was more than a poet, more than a statesman, more than a physician. We cannot understand Christ until we understand that He was the King of kings and Lord of lords. Like Thomas, our only response must be to bow down and confess, "My Lord and my God!" (John 20:28).

BILLY GRAHAM
Hope for Each Day [13]

20 MEDIATOR

For there is one God and one mediator between God and men, the man Christ Jesus.

1 TIMOTHY 2:5

*M*ediator was a concept derived from ceremonial worship prescribed by God in the Old Testament. In the temple, priests mediated between God and the Israelites by offering animal sacrifices to atone for the sins of the people and by interceding to God for the nation. In their position as mediator, the priests were the only ones eligible to enter the Holy place, the place where God made His presence known. When Jesus came to us as the Son of God and shed His blood on the cross for our sins, He became our High Priest. He is the Mediator of the New Covenant by means of His death for the redemption of our transgressions, that we might obtain forgiveness and receive the promise of eternal inheritance with God. There is only one way to Him—through the Mediator, Jesus Christ—who has the full nature of God and the full nature of man.

JACK COUNTRYMAN

21   SAVIOR

Today your Savior was born in the town of David. He is Christ, the Lord.

Luke 2:11 NCV

An ordinary night with ordinary sheep and ordinary shepherds. And were it not for a God who loves to hook an "extra" on the front of ordinary, the night would have gone unnoticed. The sheep would have been forgotten, and the shepherds would have slept the night away.

But God dances amidst the common. And that night he did a waltz.

The black sky exploded with brightness. Trees that had been shadows jumped into clarity. Sheep that had been silent became a chorus of curiosity. One minute the shepherd was dead asleep, the next he was rubbing his eyes and staring into the face of an alien. The night was ordinary no more.

The angel came in the night because that is when lights are best seen and that is when they are most needed. God comes into the common for the same reason. His most powerful tools are the simplest.

Max Lucado
The Applause of Heaven[14]

22 MY BELOVED SON

While he was still speaking, behold, a bright cloud
overshadowed them; and suddenly a voice came out of the
cloud, saying, "This is My beloved Son, in whom I am well
pleased. Hear Him!"

MATTHEW 17:5

God the Father loved Jesus the Son and publicly stated His pleasure in Christ's righteous manner of living. Jesus was totally obedient to the Father even unto death. God sent His Son to the cross on our behalf to provide for us a propitiation for our sin and a direct access to our Father God. Through this Scripture we are invited to "hear Him." Jesus, through the Holy Spirit, wishes to be our guide through life. As Jesus was in total obedience to the Father, our lives need to acknowledge Him and listen to that small, still voice that is ever-present for those who are followers of Jesus Christ.

JACK COUNTRYMAN

23 THE WAY, TRUTH, AND LIFE

I am the way, the truth, and the life.

JOHN 14:6

When we become a friend of Jesus, something revolutionary happens inside us. Our spirits, our hearts, our souls, our perspectives on life, and our capacities to love all change dramatically. We become a "New Creation."

Jesus gives to us something far more valuable than any human friend can ever give: He reveals to us the truth about God . . . the truth about ourselves . . . the truth about the relationship He desires for us to have with other human beings.

He reveals in His own presence within us the whole truth, and nothing but the truth. He is Truth.

CHARLES F. STANLEY
God's Way Day by Day[15]

24   LAMB OF GOD

The next day John saw Jesus coming toward him, and said, "Behold! The Lamb of God who takes away the sin of the world!"

JOHN 1:29

In the Old Testament, the Israelites sacrificed lambs at the Passover feast as an offering for their sins. Jesus Christ is the Lamb that God gave us as a sacrifice for sins not only for Israel but for the whole world. No one else could be God's Lamb. He was the voluntary offering. What can we do? Believe it, accept it, take our place with Him, behold Him every day, and count nothing as too inadequate or too little for Him. May each day bring you to the throne of Grace with an open heart to the leading of the Holy Spirit in everything you do. Let us be reminded that this vivid description of Jesus was a pointed announcement of the Atonement He would bring about on our behalf that we might have eternal life with our Heavenly Father.

JACK COUNTRYMAN

25 GOOD SHEPHERD

I am the good shepherd. I know my sheep, and my sheep know
me. . . .

JOHN 10:14 NCV

*T*he shepherd knows his sheep. He calls them by name.
When we see a crowd, we see exactly that, a crowd. . . .
We see people, not persons, but people. A herd of humans. A
flock of faces. That's what we see.

But not so with the Shepherd. To him every face is different. Every face is a story. Every face is a child. Every child has a
name. . . .

The shepherd knows his sheep. He knows each one by name.
The Shepherd knows you. He knows your name. And he will
never forget it.

MAX LUCADO
When God Whispers Your Name[16]

26 BREAD OF LIFE

I am the bread of life.

JOHN 6:35

*J*esus came to the world so we could know, once and for all, that God is concerned about the way we live, the way we believe, and the way we die.

God could have told us in other ways, of course—and He had, throughout the pages of the Old Testament and in the lives of His people. By His written Word He declared His love.

But Jesus was the Living Word. By His life, death, and resurrection, Jesus *demonstrated* God's love in a way we could never deny. Paul wrote, "But God demonstrates His own love toward us, in that while we were still sinners, Christ died for us" (Romans 5:8).

Every time He fed the hungry, He was saying, "I am the bread of life." Every time He healed a suffering person, He was saying, "It hurts Me to see you in pain." Every move He made, every miracle He performed, every word He spoke was for the purpose of reconciling a lost world to the loving, compassionate God.

BILLY GRAHAM
Hope for Each Day[17]

$\frac{3}{2}$ | 27   WORD

The Word became flesh and blood,
and moved into the neighborhood.

JOHN 1:14 MSG

I've always perceived the apostle John as a fellow who viewed life simply. "Right is right and wrong is wrong, and things aren't nearly as complicated as we make them out to be."

For example, defining Jesus would be a challenge to the best of writers, but John handles the task with casual analogy. The Messiah, in a word, was "the Word." A walking message. A love letter. Be He a fiery verb or a tender adjective, He was, quite simply, a word.

And life? Well, life is divided into two sections, light and darkness. If you are in one, you are not in the other and vice versa.

Next question?

MAX LUCADO
No Wonder They Call Him the Savior[18]

28 ALPHA & OMEGA

> "I am the Alpha and the Omega," says the Lord God, "who is, and who was, and who is to come, the Almighty."
>
> REVELATION 1:8 NIV

This title describes the eternal omniscience of Jesus Christ. The alpha is the first letter and the omega is the last letter in the Greek alphabet. Through the alphabet all of our words, all of our wisdom, and all of our knowledge are expressed. Jesus is the beginning and the end of the alphabet, the summation of all wisdom and knowledge.

What does the omniscience of Christ mean to me personally? It means I have always been on His mind. Think of it: The most important Man in the universe has always been thinking of you! Wonder of wonders! You have never been out of His thoughts! Even as He hung on the cross, He was thinking of you by name! Dying for you by name! And when He was raised from the dead on that first Easter Sunday, He was raised with you on His mind!

ANNE GRAHAM LOTZ
The Vision of His Glory [19]

29 RESURRECTION

> I am the resurrection and the life. He who believes in me will
> live, even though he dies.
>
> JOHN 11:25 NIV

H er words were full of despair. "If you had been here . . ." She stares into the Master's face with confused eyes. She'd been strong long enough; now it hurt too badly. Lazarus was dead. Her brother was gone. And the one man who could have made a difference didn't. He hadn't even made it for the burial. Something about death makes us accuse God of betrayal. "If God were here there would be no death!" we claim.

You see, if God is God anywhere, He has to be God in the face of death. Pop psychology can deal with depression. Pep talks can deal with pessimism. Prosperity can handle hunger. But only God can deal with our ultimate dilemma—death. And only the God of the Bible has dared to stand on the canyon's edge and offer an answer. He has to be God in the face of death. If not, He is not God anywhere.

MAX LUCADO
God Came Near [20]

30   MESSIAH

The woman said to Him, "I know that Messiah is coming" (who is called Christ). "When He comes, He will tell us all things."

JOHN 4:25

Throughout history the Jewish people had looked forward to the coming of the Messiah, the anointed one by God. He was to give them the Spirit of Life and hope that the Samaritan woman's lips bore. May our lips today bear a convincing, convicting, and converting testimony of the saving grace of the living Christ. May this Christmas bring to light the coming of the Messiah to show each of us the love and sacrifice of Jesus Christ. May we share with Him life eternal and experience, through His love, the joy and peace that comes with knowing Christ as our personal Savior.

JACK COUNTRYMAN

HALLELUJAH CHORUS

from Handel's Messiah

Hallelujah! Hallelujah! Hallelujah!
Hallelujah! Hallelujah!
For the Lord God omnipotent reigneth.
Hallelujah! Hallelujah! Hallelujah! Hallelujah!

For the Lord God omnipotent reigneth.
Hallelujah! Hallelujah! Hallelujah! Hallelujah!
Hallelujah! Hallelujah! Hallelujah!

The kingdom of this world
Is become the kingdom of our Lord,
And of His Christ, and of His Christ;
And He shall reign forever and ever,
Forever and ever, forever and ever,

King of kings, and Lord of lords,
King of kings, and Lord of lords,
And Lord of lords,
And He shall reign,
And He shall reign forever and ever,
King of kings, forever and ever,
And Lord of lords,
Hallelujah! Hallelujah!

And He shall reign forever and ever,
King of kings! and Lord of lords!
And He shall reign forever and ever,
King of kings! and Lord of lords!
Hallelujah! Hallelujah! Hallelujah!
Hallelujah! Hallelujah!

GEORGE FREDERIC HANDEL (1695–1759)

NOTES

1. *Hope for Each Day*, Billy Graham, p. 384. (Nashville, TN: Thomas Nelson, Inc., 2002).

2. *God's Way Day by Day,* Charles F. Stanley, p. 380. (Nashville, TN: Thomas Nelson, Inc., 2004).

3. *The Joy of My Heart*; Anne Graham Lotz, p. 386. Originally from *God's Story*, (Nashville, TN: W Publishing, 1997).

4. *God's Way Day by Day,* Charles F. Stanley, p. 358. (Nashville, TN: Thomas Nelson, Inc., 2004).

5. *Grace for the Moment,* Max Lucado, p. 692. Originally from *A Gentle Thunder* (Nashville, TN: Word, 1995).

6. *Discovering God's Daily Agenda,* Henry & Richard Blackaby, p. 382. (Nashville, TN: Thomas Nelson, Inc., 2007).

7. *Grace for the Moment,* Max Lucado, p. 740. Originally from *In the Grip of Grace* (Nashville, TN: Word, 1996).

8. *Truth for Today*, John MacArthur, p. 386. (Nashville, TN: JCountryman, 2001).

9. *Grace for the Moment*, Max Lucado, p. 749. Originally from *Cure for the Common Life* (Nashville, TN: W Publishing Group, 2005).

10. *Hope for Each Day*, Billy Graham, p. 376. (Nashville, TN: Thomas Nelson, Inc., 2002).

11. *Discovering God's Daily Agenda*, Henry & Richard Blackaby, p. 388. (Nashville, TN: Thomas Nelson, Inc., 2007).

12. *The Joy of My Heart*; Anne Graham Lotz, p. 257. Originally from *Just Give Me Jesus*, (Nashville, TN: W Publishing, 2002).

13. *Hope for Each Day*, Billy Graham, p. 383. (Nashville, TN: Thomas Nelson, Inc., 2002).

14. *Grace for the Moment*, Max Lucado, p. 742.Originally from *The Applause of Heaven* (Nashville, TN: Word, 1990).

15. *God's Way Day by Day*, Charles F. Stanley, p. 38. (Nashville, TN: Thomas Nelson, Inc., 2004).

16. *Grace for the Moment*, Max Lucado, p. 728. Originally from *When God Whispers Your Name* (Nashville, TN: Word, 1994).

17. *Hope for Each Day*, Billy Graham, p. 377. (Nashville, TN: Thomas Nelson, Inc., 2002).

18. *Grace for the Moment*, Max Lucado, p. 655. Originally from *No Wonder They Call Him the Savior* (Nashville, TN: W Publishing Group, 2003).

19. *The Joy of My Heart*; Anne Graham Lotz, p. 359. Originally from *The Vision of His Glory*, (Nashville, TN: W Publishing, 1996)

20. *Grace for the Moment*, Max Lucado, p. 649. Originally from *God Came Near* (Nashville, TN: W Publishing Group, 2003).

ATTRIBUTES OF GOD

| PART 3 |

PROMISES
of GOD

1 | JESUS IS YOUR SAVIOR

Not by works of righteousness which we have done, but according to His mercy He saved us, through the washing of regeneration and renewing of the Holy Spirit, whom He poured out on us abundantly through Jesus Christ our Savior.

TITUS 3:5–6

And we have seen and testify that the Father has sent the Son as Savior of the world.

1 JOHN 4:14

And my spirit has rejoiced in God my Savior.

LUKE 1:47

"For we ourselves have heard Him and we know that this is indeed the Christ, the Savior of the world."

JOHN 4:42b

"For the Son of Man has come to seek and to save that which was lost."

LUKE 19:10

Nevertheless He saved them for His name's sake,
That He might make His mighty power known.

PSALM 106:8

For God so loved the world that He gave His only begotten Son, that whoever believes in Him should not perish but have everlasting life.

JOHN 3:16

Being justified freely by His grace through the redemption that is in Christ Jesus, whom God set forth as a propitiation by His blood, through faith, to demonstrate His righteousness, because in His forbearance God had passed over the sins that were previously committed.

ROMANS 3:24–25

"Most assuredly, I say to you, he who believes in Me has everlasting life."

JOHN 6:47

For by grace you have been saved through faith, and that not of yourselves; it is the gift of God, not of works, lest anyone should boast.

EPHESIANS 2:8–9

If you confess with your mouth the Lord Jesus and believe in your heart that God has raised Him from the dead, you will be saved.

ROMANS 10:9

Therefore, if anyone is in Christ, he is a new creation; old things have passed away; behold, all things have become new.

2 CORINTHIANS 5:17

Share with me in the sufferings for the gospel according to the power of God, who has saved us and called us with a holy calling, not according to our works, but according to His own purpose and grace which was given to us in Christ Jesus before time began.

2 TIMOTHY 1:8b–9

12 JESUS IS YOUR LORD

Therefore God also has highly exalted Him and given Him the name which is above every name, that at the name of Jesus every knee should bow, of those in heaven, and of those on earth, and of those under the earth, and that every tongue should confess that Jesus Christ is Lord, to the glory of God the Father.

PHILIPPIANS 2:9–11

If you confess with your mouth the Lord Jesus and believe in your heart that God has raised Him from the dead, you will be saved. For with the heart one believes unto righteousness, and with the mouth confession is made unto salvation.

ROMANS 10:9–10

For sin shall not have dominion over you, for you are not under law but under grace.

What then? Shall we sin because we are not under law but under grace? Certainly not! Do you not know that to whom you present yourselves slaves to obey, you are that one's slaves whom you obey, whether of sin leading to death, or of obedience leading to righteousness?

ROMANS 6:14–16

"But why do you call Me 'Lord, Lord,' and not do the things which I say?"

LUKE 6:46

I beseech you therefore, brethren, by the mercies of God, that you present your bodies a living sacrifice, holy, acceptable to God, which is your reasonable service. And do not be conformed to this world, but be transformed by the renewing of your mind, that you may prove what is that good and acceptable and perfect will of God.

ROMANS 12:1–2

Or do you not know that your body is the temple of the Holy Spirit who is in you, whom you have from God, and you are not your own? For you were bought at a price; therefore glorify God in your body and in your spirit, which are God's.

1 CORINTHIANS 6:19–20

"Therefore let all the house of Israel know assuredly that God has made this Jesus, whom you crucified, both Lord and Christ."

ACTS 2:36

For if we live, we live to the Lord; and if we die, we die to the Lord. Therefore, whether we live or die, we are the Lord's.

ROMANS 14:8

For You, Lord, are good, and ready to forgive,
And abundant in mercy to all those who call upon You.

PSALM 86:5

Blessed be the Lord,
Who daily loads us with benefits,
The God of our salvation! Selah

PSALM 68:19

But it is good for me to draw near to God;
I have put my trust in the Lord GOD,
That I may declare all Your works.

PSALM 73:28

"For the Lord GOD will help Me;
Therefore I will not be disgraced;
Therefore I have set My face like a flint,
And I know that I will not be ashamed."

ISAIAH 50:7

" 'And you shall love the LORD your God with all your heart, with all your soul, with all your mind, and with all your strength.' This is the first commandment."

MARK 12:30

"For David says concerning Him:

'I foresaw the LORD always before my face,
For He is at my right hand, that I may not be shaken.' "

ACTS 2:25

3 JESUS IS YOUR LOVE

God demonstrates His own love toward us, in that while we were still sinners, Christ died for us.

ROMANS 5:8

Beloved, let us love one another, for love is of God; and everyone who loves is born of God and knows God. He who does not love does not know God, for God is love. In this the love of God was manifested toward us, that God has sent His only begotten Son into the world, that we might live through Him. In this is love, not that we loved God, but that He loved us and sent His Son to be the propitiation for our sins. Beloved, if God so loved us, we also ought to love one another.

1 JOHN 4:7–11

"As the Father loved Me, I also have loved you; abide in My love. If you keep My commandments, you will abide in My love, just as I have kept My Father's commandments and abide in His love.

"These things I have spoken to you, that My joy may remain in you, and that your joy may be full. This is My commandment, that you love one another as I have loved you. Greater love has no one than this, than to lay down one's life for his friends."

"These things I command you, that you love one another."

JOHN 15:9–13, 17

I bow my knees to the Father of our Lord Jesus Christ . . . that He would grant you, according to the riches of His glory, to be strengthened with might through His Spirit in the inner man, that Christ may dwell in your hearts through faith; that you, being rooted and grounded in love, may be able to comprehend with all the saints what is the width and length and depth and height—to know the love of Christ which passes knowledge; that you may be filled with all the fullness of God.

EPHESIANS 3:14, 16–19

We have known and believed the love that God has for us. God is love, and he who abides in love abides in God, and God in him. . . .
We love Him because He first loved us.

1 JOHN 4:16, 19

I love those who love me,
And those who seek me diligently will find me.

PROVERBS 8:17

The LORD has appeared of old to me, saying:
"Yes, I have loved you with an everlasting love;
Therefore with lovingkindness I have drawn you."

JEREMIAH 31:3

For God so loved the world that He gave His only begotten Son, that whoever believes in Him should not perish but have everlasting life.

JOHN 3:16

PROMISES OF GOD

"I will betroth you to Me forever;
Yes, I will betroth you to Me
In righteousness and justice,
In lovingkindness and mercy;
I will betroth you to Me in faithfulness,
And you shall know the LORD."

HOSEA 2:19–20

"He who has My commandments and keeps them, it is he who loves Me. And he who loves Me will be loved by My Father, and I will love him and manifest Myself to him."

JOHN 14:21

The LORD will command His lovingkindness in the daytime,
And in the night His song shall be with me—
A prayer to the God of my life.

PSALM 42:8

And now abide faith, hope, love, these three; but the greatest of these is love.

1 CORINTHIANS 13:13

For I am persuaded that neither death nor life, nor angels nor principalities nor powers, nor things present nor things to come, nor height nor depth, nor any other created thing, shall be able to separate us from the love of God which is in Christ Jesus our Lord.

ROMANS 8:38–39

4 JESUS IS YOUR PEACE

You will keep him in perfect peace,
Whose mind is stayed on You,
Because he trusts in You.

ISAIAH 26:3

But now in Christ Jesus you who once were far off have been brought near by the blood of Christ.

For He Himself is our peace, who has made both one, and has broken down the middle wall of separation.

EPHESIANS 2:13–14

Be anxious for nothing, but in everything by prayer and supplication, with thanksgiving, let your requests be made known to God; and the peace of God, which surpasses all understanding, will guard your hearts and minds through Christ Jesus.

PHILIPPIANS 4:6–7

LORD, You will establish peace for us,
For You have also done all our works in us.

ISAIAH 26:12

For unto us a Child is born,

Unto us a Son is given;

And the government will be upon His shoulder.

And His name will be called

Wonderful, Counselor, Mighty God,

Everlasting Father, Prince of Peace.

Of the increase of His government and peace

There will be no end,

Upon the throne of David and over His kingdom,

To order it and establish it with judgment and justice

From that time forward, even forever.

The zeal of the Lord of hosts will perform this.

ISAIAH 9:6–7

And the God of peace will crush Satan under your feet shortly.

The grace of our Lord Jesus Christ be with you. Amen.

ROMANS 16:20

The things which you learned and received and heard and saw in me,

these do, and the God of peace will be with you.

PHILIPPIANS 4:9

Therefore, having been justified by faith, we have peace with God

through our Lord Jesus Christ.

ROMANS 5:1

And let the peace of God rule in your hearts, to which also you were called in one body; and be thankful.

COLOSSIANS 3:15

I will both lie down in peace, and sleep;
For You alone, O LORD, make me dwell in safety.

PSALM 4:8

The LORD will give strength to His people;
The LORD will bless His people with peace.

PSALM 29:11

Peace I leave with you, My peace I give to you; not as the world gives do I give to you. Let not your heart be troubled, neither let it be afraid.

JOHN 14:27

5 JESUS IS YOUR FORGIVENESS

To the praise of the glory of His grace, by which He made us accepted in the Beloved.

In Him we have redemption through His blood, the forgiveness of sins, according to the riches of His grace.

EPHESIANS 1:6–7

You have forgiven the iniquity of Your people;
You have covered all their sin. Selah

PSALM 85:2

Therefore, if anyone is in Christ, he is a new creation; old things have passed away; behold, all things have become new.

2 CORINTHIANS 5:17

As far as the east is from the west,
So far has He removed our transgressions from us.

PSALM 103:12

My little children, these things I write to you, so that you may not sin. And if anyone sins, we have an Advocate with the Father, Jesus Christ the righteous.

1 JOHN 2:1

If we confess our sins, He is faithful and just to forgive us our sins and to cleanse us from all unrighteousness.

1 JOHN 1:9

"For I will be merciful to their unrighteousness, and their sins and their lawless deeds I will remember no more."

HEBREWS 8:12

> Let the wicked forsake his way,
> And the unrighteous man his thoughts;
> Let him return to the LORD,
> And He will have mercy on him;
> And to our God,
> For He will abundantly pardon.

ISAIAH 55:7

Bearing with one another, and forgiving one another, if anyone has a complaint against another; even as Christ forgave you, so you also must do.

COLOSSIANS 3:13

"And whenever you stand praying, if you have anything against anyone, forgive him, that your Father in heaven may also forgive you your trespasses."

MARK 11:25

And you, being dead in your trespasses and the uncircumcision of your flesh, He has made alive together with Him, having forgiven you all trespasses.

COLOSSIANS 2:13

I will cleanse them from all their iniquity by which they have sinned against Me, and I will pardon all their iniquities by which they have sinned and by which they have transgressed against Me.

JEREMIAH 33:8

"Come now, and let us reason together,"
Says the LORD,
"Though your sins are like scarlet,
They shall be as white as snow;
Though they are red like crimson,
They shall be as wool."

ISAIAH 1:18

"I, even I, am He who blots out your transgressions for My
    own sake;
And I will not remember your sins."

ISAIAH 43:25

6 JESUS IS YOUR RIGHTEOUSNESS

For He made Him who knew no sin to be sin for us, that we might become the righteousness of God in Him.

2 CORINTHIANS 5:21

But of Him you are in Christ Jesus, who became for us wisdom from God—and righteousness and sanctification and redemption.

1 CORINTHIANS 1:30

And be found in Him, not having my own righteousness, which is from the law, but that which is through faith in Christ, the righteousness which is from God by faith.

PHILIPPIANS 3:9

Just as Abraham "believed God, and it was accounted to him for righteousness." Therefore know that only those who are of faith are sons of Abraham.

GALATIANS 3:6–7

Even the righteousness of God, through faith in Jesus Christ, to all and on all who believe. For there is no difference.

ROMANS 3:22

Being justified freely by His grace through the redemption that is in Christ Jesus, whom God set forth as a propitiation by His blood, through faith, to demonstrate His righteousness, because in His forbearance God had passed over the sins that were previously committed, to demonstrate at the present time His righteousness, that He might be just and the justifier of the one who has faith in Jesus.

ROMANS 3:24–26

In righteousness you shall be established;
You shall be far from oppression, for you shall not fear;
And from terror, for it shall not come near you.
Indeed they shall surely assemble, but not because of Me.
Whoever assembles against you shall fall for your sake.

"Behold, I have created the blacksmith
Who blows the coals in the fire,
Who brings forth an instrument for his work;
And I have created the spoiler to destroy.
No weapon formed against you shall prosper,
And every tongue which rises against you in judgment
You shall condemn.
This is the heritage of the servants of the LORD,
And their righteousness is from Me,"
Says the LORD.

ISAIAH 54:14–17

But to him who does not work but believes on Him who justifies the ungodly, his faith is accounted for righteousness.

Romans 4:5

For what the law could not do in that it was weak through the flesh, God did by sending His own Son in the likeness of sinful flesh, on account of sin: He condemned sin in the flesh, that the righteous requirement of the law might be fulfilled in us who do not walk according to the flesh but according to the Spirit.

Romans 8:3–4

Not by works of righteousness which we have done, but according to His mercy He saved us, through the washing of regeneration and renewing of the Holy Spirit.

Titus 3:5

For if by the one man's offense death reigned through the one, much more those who receive abundance of grace and of the gift of righteousness will reign in life through the One, Jesus Christ.

Romans 5:17

What shall we say then? That Gentiles, who did not pursue righteousness, have attained to righteousness, even the righteousness of faith.

Romans 9:30

7 | JESUS IS YOUR DELIVERER

"The Spirit of the Lord GOD is upon Me,

Because the LORD has anointed Me

To preach good tidings to the poor;

He has sent Me to heal the brokenhearted,

To proclaim liberty to the captives,

And the opening of the prison to those who are bound.

ISAIAH 61:1

"And you shall know the truth, and the truth shall make you free." . . .

"Therefore if the Son makes you free, you shall be free indeed."

JOHN 8:32, 36

For the law of the Spirit of life in Christ Jesus has made me free from the law of sin and death.

ROMANS 8:2

Behold, I give you the authority to trample on serpents and scorpions, and over all the power of the enemy, and nothing shall by any means hurt you.

LUKE 10:19

Now the Lord is the Spirit; and where the Spirit of the Lord is, there is liberty.

2 CORINTHIANS 3:17

But now having been set free from sin, and having become slaves of God, you have your fruit to holiness, and the end, everlasting life.

ROMANS 6:22

> For You have broken the yoke of his burden
> And the staff of his shoulder,
> The rod of his oppressor,
> As in the day of Midian.

ISAIAH 9:4

> "The Spirit of the LORD is upon Me,
> Because He has anointed Me
> to preach the gospel to the poor;
> He has sent Me to heal the brokenhearted,
> To proclaim liberty to the captives
> And recovery of sight to the blind,
> To set at liberty those who are oppressed."

LUKE 4:18

And these signs will follow those who believe: In My name they will cast out demons; they will speak with new tongues.

MARK 16:17

And they overcame him by the blood of the Lamb and by the word of their testimony, and they did not love their lives to the death.

REVELATION 12:11

8 JESUS IS YOUR FELLOWSHIP

That which we have seen and heard we declare to you, that you also may have fellowship with us; and truly our fellowship is with the Father and with His Son Jesus Christ.

1 JOHN 1:3

God is faithful, by whom you were called into the fellowship of His Son, Jesus Christ our Lord.

1 CORINTHIANS 1:9

Behold, I stand at the door and knock. If anyone hears My voice and opens the door, I will come in to him and dine with him, and he with Me.

REVELATION 3:20

Jesus answered and said to him, "If anyone loves Me, he will keep My word; and My Father will love him, and We will come to him and make Our home with him."

JOHN 14:23

"Sing and rejoice, O daughter of Zion! For behold, I am coming and I will dwell in your midst," says the LORD.

ZECHARIAH 2:10

"He who has My commandments and keeps them, it is he who loves Me. And he who loves Me will be loved by My Father, and I will love him and manifest Myself to him."

JOHN 14:21

"Abide in Me, and I in you. As the branch cannot bear fruit of itself, unless it abides in the vine, neither can you, unless you abide in Me.

"I am the vine, you are the branches. He who abides in Me, and I in him, bears much fruit; for without Me you can do nothing. . . . If you abide in Me, and My words abide in you, you will ask what you desire, and it shall be done for you."

JOHN 15:4–5, 7

Therefore if there is any consolation in Christ, if any comfort of love, if any fellowship of the Spirit, if any affection and mercy, fulfill my joy by being like-minded, having the same love, being of one accord, of one mind.

PHILIPPIANS 2:1–2

"For where two or three are gathered together in My name, I am there in the midst of them."

MATTHEW 18:20

I am a companion of all who fear You,
And of those who keep Your precepts.

PSALM 119:63

And walk in love, as Christ also has loved us and given Himself for us, an offering and a sacrifice to God for a sweet-smelling aroma. . . .

Be filled with the Spirit, speaking to one another in psalms and hymns and spiritual songs, singing and making melody in your heart to the Lord. . . .

For we are members of His body, of His flesh and of His bones.

EPHESIANS 5:2, 18b–19, 30

This is the message which we have heard from Him and declare to you, that God is light and in Him is no darkness at all. If we say that we have fellowship with Him, and walk in darkness, we lie and do not practice the truth. But if we walk in the light as He is in the light, we have fellowship with one another, and the blood of Jesus Christ His Son cleanses us from all sin.

1 JOHN 1:5–7

9 JESUS IS YOUR EXAMPLE

For to this you were called, because Christ also suffered for us, leaving us an example, that you should follow His steps.

1 PETER 2:21

Therefore be imitators of God as dear children. And walk in love, as Christ also has loved us and given Himself for us, an offering and a sacrifice to God for a sweet-smelling aroma.

EPHESIANS 5:1–2

Let this mind be in you which was also in Christ Jesus, who, being in the form of God, did not consider it robbery to be equal with God, but made Himself of no reputation, taking the form of a bondservant, and coming in the likeness of men. And being found in appearance as a man, He humbled Himself and became obedient to the point of death, even the death of the cross.

PHILIPPIANS 2:5–8

"Yet it shall not be so among you; but whoever desires to become great among you shall be your servant. And whoever of you desires to be first shall be slave of all. For even the Son of Man did not come to be served, but to serve, and to give His life a ransom for many."

MARK 10:43–45

"If I then, your Lord and Teacher, have washed your feet, you also ought to wash one another's feet. For I have given you an example, that you should do as I have done to you."

JOHN 13:14–15

He who says he abides in Him ought himself also to walk just as He walked.

1 JOHN 2:6

"A new commandment I give to you, that you love one another; as I have loved you, that you also love one another."

JOHN 13:34

By this we know love, because He laid down His life for us. And we also ought to lay down our lives for the brethren.

1 JOHN 3:16

Now may the God of patience and comfort grant you to be like-minded toward one another, according to Christ Jesus, that you may with one mind and one mouth glorify the God and Father of our Lord Jesus Christ.

Therefore receive one another, just as Christ also received us, to the glory of God.

ROMANS 15:5–7

Bearing with one another, and forgiving one another, if anyone has a complaint against another; even as Christ forgave you, so you also must do.

COLOSSIANS 3:13

10 JESUS IS YOUR COMPANION

I am a companion of all who fear You,
And of those who keep Your precepts.

PSALM 119:63

A man who has friends must himself be friendly,
But there is a friend who sticks closer than a brother.

PROVERBS 18:24

Let your conduct be without covetousness; be content with such things as you have. For He Himself has said, "I will never leave you nor forsake you."

HEBREWS 13:5

"No longer do I call you servants, for a servant does not know what his master is doing; but I have called you friends, for all things that I heard from My Father I have made known to you. You did not choose Me, but I chose you and appointed you that you should go and bear fruit, and that your fruit should remain, that whatever you ask the Father in My name He may give you."

JOHN 15:15–16

"I will not leave you orphans; I will come to you."

JOHN 14:18

But if we walk in the light as He is in the light, we have fellowship with one another, and the blood of Jesus Christ His Son cleanses us from all sin.

1 John 1:7

> "For the mountains shall depart
> And the hills be removed,
> But My kindness shall not depart from you,
> Nor shall My covenant of peace be removed,"
> Says the Lord, who has mercy on you.

Isaiah 54:10

Behold, I stand at the door and knock. If anyone hears My voice and opens the door, I will come in to him and dine with him, and he with Me.

Revelation 3:20

Draw near to God and He will draw near to you. Cleanse your hands, you sinners; and purify your hearts, you double-minded.

James 4:8

"This is My commandment, that you love one another as I have loved you. Greater love has no one than this, than to lay down one's life for his friends. You are My friends if you do whatever I command you."

John 15:12–14

11 JESUS IS YOUR BROTHER

"For whoever does the will of My Father in heaven is My brother and sister and mother."

MATTHEW 12:50

For both He who sanctifies and those who are being sanctified are all of one, for which reason He is not ashamed to call them brethren.

HEBREWS 2:11

For whom He foreknew, He also predestined to be conformed to the image of His Son, that He might be the firstborn among many brethren.

ROMANS 8:29

For you are all sons of God through faith in Christ Jesus.

GALATIANS 3:26

But as many as received Him, to them He gave the right to become children of God, to those who believe in His name.

JOHN 1:12

Now, therefore, you are no longer strangers and foreigners, but fellow citizens with the saints and members of the household of God.

EPHESIANS 2:19

Behold what manner of love the Father has bestowed on us, that we should be called children of God! Therefore the world does not know us, because it did not know Him.

1 JOHN 3:1

And because you are sons, God has sent forth the Spirit of His Son into your hearts, crying out, "Abba, Father!" Therefore you are no longer a slave but a son, and if a son, then an heir of God through Christ.

GALATIANS 4:6–7

For as many as are led by the Spirit of God, these are sons of God.

ROMANS 8:14

Beloved, now we are children of God; and it has not yet been revealed what we shall be, but we know that when He is revealed, we shall be like Him, for we shall see Him as He is.

1 JOHN 3:2

12 JESUS IS YOUR SECURITY

Blessed be the God and Father of our Lord Jesus Christ, who according to His abundant mercy has begotten us again to a living hope through the resurrection of Jesus Christ from the dead, to an inheritance incorruptible and undefiled and that does not fade away, reserved in heaven for you, who are kept by the power of God through faith for salvation ready to be revealed in the last time.

1 PETER 1:3–5

"My sheep hear My voice, and I know them, and they follow Me. And I give them eternal life, and they shall never perish; neither shall anyone snatch them out of My hand. My Father, who has given them to Me, is greater than all; and no one is able to snatch them out of My Father's hand."

JOHN 10:27–29

For I am persuaded that neither death nor life, nor angels nor principalities nor powers, nor things present nor things to come, nor height nor depth, nor any other created thing, shall be able to separate us from the love of God which is in Christ Jesus our Lord.

ROMANS 8:38–39

Being confident of this very thing, that He who has begun a good work in you will complete it until the day of Jesus Christ.

PHILIPPIANS 1:6

But the Lord is faithful, who will establish you and guard you from the evil one.

2 THESSALONIANS 3:3

Who also has sealed us and given us the Spirit in our hearts as a guarantee.

2 CORINTHIANS 1:22

Now to Him who is able to keep you from stumbling,
And to present you faultless
Before the presence of His glory with exceeding joy,
To God our Savior,
Who alone is wise,
Be glory and majesty,
Dominion and power,
Both now and forever.
Amen.

JUDE 24–25

Lift up your eyes on high,
And see who has created these things,
Who brings out their host by number;
He calls them all by name,
By the greatness of His might
And the strength of His power;
Not one is missing.

ISAIAH 40:26

Surely goodness and mercy shall follow me
All the days of my life;
And I will dwell in the house of the LORD
Forever.

PSALM 23:6

"Do not labor for the food which perishes, but for the food which endures to everlasting life, which the Son of Man will give you, because God the Father has set His seal on Him."

JOHN 6:27

In Him you also trusted, after you heard the word of truth, the gospel of your salvation; in whom also, having believed, you were sealed with the Holy Spirit of promise.

EPHESIANS 1:13

And do not grieve the Holy Spirit of God, by whom you were sealed for the day of redemption.

EPHESIANS 4:30

"All that the Father gives Me will come to Me, and the one who comes to Me I will by no means cast out."

JOHN 6:37

PROMISES OF GOD

And we desire that each one of you show the same diligence to the full assurance of hope until the end, that you do not become sluggish, but imitate those who through faith and patience inherit the promises. . . . that by two immutable things, in which it is impossible for God to lie, we might have strong consolation, who have fled for refuge to lay hold of the hope set before us.

This hope we have as an anchor of the soul, both sure and steadfast, and which enters the Presence behind the veil, where the forerunner has entered for us, even Jesus, having become High Priest forever according to the order of Melchizedek.

HEBREWS 6:11–12, 18–20

13 JESUS IS YOUR SUFFICIENCY

And God is able to make all grace abound toward you, that you, always having all sufficiency in all things, may have an abundance for every good work.

2 CORINTHIANS 9:8

And my God shall supply all your need according to His riches in glory by Christ Jesus.

PHILIPPIANS 4:19

"Therefore I say to you, whatever things you ask when you pray, believe that you receive them, and you will have them."

MARK 11:24

Not that we are sufficient of ourselves to think of anything as being from ourselves, but our sufficiency is from God.

2 CORINTHIANS 3:5

I can do all things through Christ who strengthens me.

PHILIPPIANS 4:13

And what is the exceeding greatness of His power toward us who believe, according to the working of His mighty power.

EPHESIANS 1:19

And He said to me, "My grace is sufficient for you, for My strength is made perfect in weakness." Therefore most gladly I will rather boast in my infirmities, that the power of Christ may rest upon me.

2 CORINTHIANS 12:9

Yet in all these things we are more than conquerors through Him who loved us.

ROMANS 8:37

Blessed be the God and Father of our Lord Jesus Christ, who has blessed us with every spiritual blessing in the heavenly places in Christ.

EPHESIANS 1:3

"If you abide in Me, and My words abide in you, you will ask what you desire, and it shall be done for you."

JOHN 15:7

And whatever you ask in My name, that I will do, that the Father may be glorified in the Son.

JOHN 14:13

"And in that day you will ask Me nothing. Most assuredly, I say to you, whatever you ask the Father in My name He will give you. Until now you have asked nothing in My name. Ask, and you will receive, that your joy may be full."

JOHN 16:23–24

"And whatever things you ask in prayer, believing, you will receive."

MATTHEW 21:22

He who did not spare His own Son, but delivered Him up for us all, how shall He not with Him also freely give us all things?

ROMANS 8:32

As His divine power has given to us all things that pertain to life and godliness, through the knowledge of Him who called us by glory and virtue, by which have been given to us exceedingly great and precious promises, that through these you may be partakers of the divine nature, having escaped the corruption that is in the world through lust.

2 PETER 1:3–4

> Bless the LORD, O my soul,
> And forget not all His benefits:
> Who forgives all your iniquities,
> Who heals all your diseases,
> Who redeems your life from destruction,
> Who crowns you with lovingkindness and tender mercies.

PSALM 103:2–4

⸙|14 JESUS IS YOUR EVERYTHING

And my God shall supply all your need according to His riches in glory by Christ Jesus.

PHILIPPIANS 4:19

I can do all things through Christ who strengthens me.

PHILIPPIANS 4:13

Yet in all these things we are more than conquerors through Him who loved us.

ROMANS 8:37

Therefore let no one boast in men. For all things are yours: whether Paul or Apollos or Cephas, or the world or life or death, or things present or things to come—all are yours. And you are Christ's, and Christ is God's.

1 CORINTHIANS 3:21–23

> Blessed be the Lord,
> Who daily loads us with benefits,
> The God of our salvation! Selah

PSALM 68:19

"And in that day you will ask Me nothing. Most assuredly, I say to you, whatever you ask the Father in My name He will give you. Until now you have asked nothing in My name. Ask, and you will receive, that your joy may be full."

JOHN 16:23–24

"If you abide in Me, and My words abide in you, you will ask what you desire, and it shall be done for you."

JOHN 15:7

"Therefore I say to you, whatever things you ask when you pray, believe that you receive them, and you will have them."

MARK 11:24

Blessed be the God and Father of our Lord Jesus Christ, who has blessed us with every spiritual blessing in the heavenly places in Christ.

EPHESIANS 1:3

And whatever we ask we receive from Him, because we keep His commandments and do those things that are pleasing in His sight.

1 JOHN 3:22

For He made Him who knew no sin to be sin for us, that we might become the righteousness of God in Him.

2 CORINTHIANS 5:21

For to me, to live is Christ, and to die is gain.

PHILIPPIANS 1:21